slutever

slut*ever*

dispatches from a sexually
autonomous woman in a
post-shame world

KARLEY SCIORTINO

GRAND CENTRAL
PUBLISHING

NEW YORK   BOSTON

Grand Central Publishing
Hachette Book Group
1290 Avenue of the Americas, New York, NY 10104
grandcentralpublishing.com
twitter.com/grandcentralpub

First Edition: February 2018

Grand Central Publishing is a division of Hachette Book Group, Inc. The Grand Central Publishing name and logo is a trademark of Hachette Book Group, Inc.

The publisher is not responsible for websites (or their content) that are not owned by the publisher.

The Hachette Speakers Bureau provides a wide range of authors for speaking events. To find out more, go to www.hachettespeakersbureau.com or call (866) 376-6591.

Library of Congress Control Number: 2017956265

ISBN 978-1-4789-4476-8 (trade paperback)
ISBN 978-1-4789-4475-1 (ebook)

Printed in the United States of America

LSC-C

10 9 8 7 6 5 4 3 2 1

To my mother, who I love dearly, but who
I might not let read this book.

slutever

manifesto
slutting towards bethlehem

S*lut" is a great word.* It just sounds perfect—so sharp and clear and beautiful. It's one of those satisfying four-letter words, like "cunt" and "fuck." "Slut" also happens to be an anagram for "lust," which is one of those divine coincidences that makes you wonder if God actually exists.

We're lucky that "slut" is such a great word, because it's pretty safe to say that every woman will be called a slut at least once in her lifetime. I, personally, have the distinct pleasure of being called a slut like twelve times a day—just one of the many perks of being a sex writer in the age of internet trolls (*hair flip*). I'm not sure if my brain is wired wrong, or if I've simply developed a defense mechanism after years of harassment for being a professional blowjob blogger, but now when someone calls me a slut I get bizarrely excited by it. I find perverse pleasure in knowing that simply by being a woman who openly enjoys sex, I'm able to incite rage in total randoms. It's entertaining. And it's a rite of passage. Being called a slut means you've really *made it*, ya know? Like you're officially a woman.

But what is a slut, anyway? According to the relic known as the *Oxford English Dictionary*, "slut" is a pejorative term for a woman who has many sexual partners. However, in recent years, the word has gone a bit rogue. These days, it's often used maliciously as an umbrella term for any woman who's openly sexual. Something as PG-13 as texting someone a topless selfie can make you a metaphorical whore these days. But if you can be slut-shamed while you're still a virgin, then how do we define what it means to be a slut? Who holds the keys to the slut kingdom?

To me, a slut is a person who seeks out visceral experiences through sex. Being a slut is not necessarily about having a high body count; it's about being sexually activated. A slut is someone who has no moral obstacle between themselves and their desire to enjoy sex. A slut is a person who has sex with who they want, how they want, and isn't ashamed about it. Sluts are special. Sluts are radical. And sluts are also skilled at time management, because we can handle multiple dicks on rotation, plus our jobs and our blogs and our beauty routines. It's not easy, being a ho. Not everyone is qualified for this coveted position.

And the slut label is unifying. When I meet a girl who self-identifies as a slut, I immediately feel an affinity with her—like, *one of us*. It's like a modern-day vagina version of the Freemasons, except without the cool secret handshake. (Unless a hand job counts?) I believe that once we accept this more contemporary, sophisticated definition of "slut," it will be easier to accept the label as a badge of honor.

Unfortunately, much of the world has yet to catch up

to our level of slutty enlightenment. Until they do, we just
have to own it. One of the best pieces of advice my mother
ever gave me was: Whenever someone insults you, just
smile and say "thank you" in that wonderfully blasé-slash-
potentially clueless tone that Andy Warhol perfected. For
example, I was recently at the STD clinic being casually
diagnosed with throat gonorrhea when the doctor let out
an unnecessarily long sigh. "*Well*," he said condescendingly, "I've never known a *woman* to have gonorrhea in
her throat before. Usually we only see that in gay men."
And I was like, "Wow, thank you!" Followed by, "Did you
just assume my gender?"

So far, my sex life has been—how should I put
it...colorful? There've been a lot of ups and downs. And,
like, whips and chains, lies and deceit, love and hate, lust
and money. Not to mention bruises, rashes, dungeons,
confusion, insecurity, blackouts, crutches, orgies, doctor's
appointments, boys, girls, toys, trauma, hotels, jealousy,
addiction, mysterious bloodstains—ya know, the usual.

For the most part, I've found my sexual curiosity to be
a positive trait, as it's led me to have experiences that I'm
certain I'll be happy to have had when I die—from *Eyes
Wide Shut*–style sex parties in hotel penthouses, to being the "first assistant dildo" on a porn set, to somehow
ending up in a prisoner-of-war role play in Munich with a
married couple who didn't speak a word of English. Without question, if I weren't as slutty as I am, my life thus far
would have been far less interesting. As my hooker friend
likes to say: "Sluts have more fun." But my sluttiness has

also been the cause of many existential bathroom-mirror moments. Over the years, I've often found myself stabbing at the ingrown hairs on my bikini line, thinking: *How does my gang-bang fantasy factor into my life plan about who I think I am… or whatever?*

We are taught that our sexual behavior has a vital impact on who we are, our mental well-being, and how other people perceive us—*especially* for women. From a young age, society tells us that when a guy has a lot of sex, he's a virile Don Juan who's just fulfilling his biological urge to spread his seed (gross?). But if you're a woman who has a lot of sex, not only are you a slut (in a bad way), but there's also something fundamentally wrong with your brain. You couldn't possibly just want sex for fun, like guys supposedly do, so the desire must be coming from low self-esteem, depression, or because you're "ugly" and can't get a boyfriend (as if ugly people don't have boyfriends?). Talk about gaslighting on a mega-scale.

Since my teens, part of me has been infatuated with the rebelliousness of being a girl who sleeps around. But there was another part of me that thought, *Let's be real—there's probably something wrong with me.* It's hard to escape this gloomy self-diagnosis when everyone close to you—from your parents, to your church, to your friends and boyfriends and even the characters in your favorite movies—is constantly telling you that if you're a girl who has a lot of sex, it means that you're unequivocally fucked up.

In terms of sexual freedom, we've come a long way in recent years. (*Hello*, you can say "pussy" on TV now.)

But there continue to be lots of mixed messages floating around. The double standard is finally beginning to fade, but we're still a culture with a slut-shaming problem, often made worse (or at least more public) by social media. Casual sex has become a casual part of the cultural conversation—women stalk prey on dating apps just like men do—and yet it's still taboo to be a woman who has multiple partners. While many women today are vocally antislut–shaming, very few women are openly slutty. Basically, society is experiencing growing pains when it comes to female sexual autonomy. To be a slut or not to be a slut? That is the modern feminist question.

slutty heroines

It's a no-brainer that we're influenced by the people and stories that make up the culture around us. And it's difficult to cite an example, either real or fictional, of a happy, healthy, promiscuous person—let alone a woman. There's yet to be a successful woman in a movie who says, "I've got four guys on rotation and feel great about it," because that freaks people out. Usually, instead, the story goes that the slut gets punished—whether she dies in the end, or ends up miserable and alone, or is slut-shamed off campus—because that's the narrative our society is comfortable with. The promiscuous woman is painted as evil, inconsequential, or disposable. The slut doesn't get to become a lawyer and live happily ever after.

Like, have you ever noticed that in basically every horror movie ever made, the "slutty girl" is the first to get stabbed or eaten by zombies? Yeah, that's not a coincidence. The "punished slut" narrative is ubiquitous across film, TV, and literature. From classic examples like *Anna Karenina*, *Belle du Jour*, and *The Scarlet Letter* (shout out to Hester Prynne, OG high priestess of slut-shaming) to modern real-world cases like Monica Lewinsky and the Duke Porn Star, sluts have been getting fucked—literally and figuratively—since basically the dawn of time. Writer Tina Fey really hit the nail on the head in *Mean Girls*, when the high school sex-ed teacher tells his young female students: "Do not have sex. If you have sex, you will get pregnant...and die." Funny, yet morbidly on point.

While men have long been the arbiters of mass media, they are not solely to blame for the tortured-slut narrative. Women are often also complicit in slut-shaming. At the risk of sounding like I'm *prude*-shaming, it seems to me that a lot of women repress their inner slut because they think that feigning naiveté will increase their sexual or romantic value. These women are buying into the notion that overt female sexuality scares men (because men are actually more insecure about their sexuality than women), and that men need to operate under the illusion that women are clueless about sex. But this is *tragique*. When we do this, not only are we fucking shit up for womankind, but we're also hurting ourselves. It's like faking orgasms—pulling a Sally when some guy is basically setting your clit on fire means that he's going to keep doing that for eternity (or at least until a braver woman comes along and sets him straight). In my opinion, the woman who is truly perverse is the woman who pretends she's not sexual to appease a (thoroughly misguided) man.

Of course, not all women have voracious sexual appetites, or are strategically wearing ill-fitting turtlenecks to conceal their inner sex maniac. Some women just aren't interested in having a ton of sex, and to them I say: "It's weird that you're reading this book, but I respect you!" The unglamorous reality is, we live in a sex-negative society that conflates having a lot of sex with being a bad person—especially if you have a (supposedly sacred) vagina. Because of this, it can be difficult to separate our own desires (or lack thereof) from a society that tells us that a woman who sleeps around is a skanky loser. Sometimes, when it comes to sex, we end up lying to ourselves about who we are and what we want. Like, who knows—maybe you're secretly a ho, but you just haven't allowed yourself to realize it yet. (Something to look forward to.)

Thankfully, there are a few beacons of light in the otherwise slutless media. An obvious example is Samantha on *Sex and the City*, whose unapologetic, self-aware slut pride and professional success have made her the reigning queen of women with a high appetite for sex and adventure. There are porn stars like Sasha Grey and Stoya—intelligent women who promote extreme sexual exploration and also speak out about sexual health. I love Amber Rose, Amy Schumer, Rihanna, The Broad City girls, and Chelsea Handler, who all flaunt brazen, more-is-better attitudes toward sex. These women are great, but we need more like them, especially in the mainstream. Like all marginalized groups, sluts need representation, and we are seriously lacking in slutty role models. We need more smart, responsibly promiscuous women, acting as living proof that having a high sexual appetite, and satisfying it, doesn't mean you're an awful person or doomed.

Back when I first started writing about sex, one of my mother's main concerns—and there were many—was that being open about my slutty adventures online would make it difficult to find a guy to date me. And I have to admit, there was a time when I thought maybe she was right. But the reality is, if someone doesn't want to date me because I'm a slut, then he's clearly not the guy for me anyway. I don't care if some bro finds me less appealing because of how many partners I've had, or if he doesn't want to take me home to his mother, because while my lifestyle may be unattractive to him, his ideals are unattractive to me. In a way, being open about your sexuality actually acts as a filter through which only the enlightened may pass. And besides, there are plenty of sexually open-minded dudes to go around, enough to (at least attempt to) satisfy all the sluts currently roaming the planet. And if I'm wrong about that, well, we're sexually flexible Millennials—we can just become lesbians.

victim who?

If you're a sexually curious woman, along with being called a slut, another unfortunate refrain is: "Are you *sure* you want to do that?" Some of my greatest hits include: Are you *sure* you want to fuck that married couple? Are you *sure* you want to go to that sex party? Are you *sure* you want to be suspended upside down from the ceiling by a guy with a low-hanging man bun? Are you *sure* you want to pee into that lawyer's mouth for $200? The implication, of course, always being: because you might not like it! But it's like…okay, so what?

As women, we're led to believe that a negative sexual experience can be devastating—that if some asshole crosses one of our sexual boundaries, or if we leave the orgy feeling fat and uncomfortable instead of enlightened, that we might *never recover*. But why do women always have to be the "victims" of sex? Why is it that in nearly every area of our lives we are encouraged to take risks and try new things—to *Lean In* and play hard—but when it comes to sex, we're like, "Be safe or you'll end up traumatized or dead"? These doomsday ideas become self-fulfilling prophecies, cultivating a type of sexual fragility that I don't think is healthy.

It's true that sex can be high-risk. Things go wrong. People get hurt. But just because I had a bad sexual experience doesn't mean that I'm broken. It means I know to avoid that thing going forward. I've done a lot of things in my life that it turned out I didn't like—like that time, for instance, when I let my boyfriend tie me to a dresser while I watched him have sex with my best friend. Unsurprisingly, it was literally awful, but now at least I can say I've done it? The point is, there are far worse things in life than bad sex (like a hangover, for example).

Of course, sexual assault is real, and should not be tolerated under any circumstances. But assault is separate from the concept of victimhood. Feeling like a victim is a subjective headspace. Think about it this way: Men are taught that there is no such thing as a negative sexual experience. From a young age, boys are essentially taught: All sex is good sex; take what you can get; even a bad blow job is a good blow job. Pretty much the only quasi-negative sexual experience that you ever see a man have in a movie is the trope of a guy being tricked into sex with a fat or ugly woman—which, of course, is never traumatic for him, but rather a comical encounter that provides fodder for banter with his friends the next morning. But when a woman is coerced into sex, she spends the rest of the movie crying in the shower and developing a cheesy nineties-throwback self-harm habit.

It's no secret that female sexuality has long been policed. But today we've created an environment where (allegedly predatory) male sexuality needs to be policed, and (allegedly passive) female sexuality needs to be protected—which seems equally tragic to me. At the heart of the victim narrative is a familiar and unfortunate premise: the idea that, by having sex, men are *getting* something, whereas women are *giving something up*. It's outdated, it's offensive, and it's psychologically destructive for women, because it has the power to mislead girls into thinking that having one not-ideal sexual experience means that they have lost a part of themselves. *Hello—*

pitying and victimizing women doesn't help us; it just dismisses the importance of female sexual agency.

Back in the mid-1960s, universities set curfews for their female students, whereas men were allowed to stay out as late as they pleased. It was then that a faction of the feminist movement, in part lead by Camille Paglia—the controversial feminist, academic, and writer, who back then was a college student—fought to gain the same freedoms that men had. They rejected the need for special protections, instead wanting autonomy over their private lives. They said: "Give us the freedom to risk rape." Of course, that sounds jarring. But the point they were making is relevant still: We would rather be free in the world and accept whatever risk comes along with that than be trapped inside, endlessly braiding each other's hair like passive Rapunzels.

In our postwoke social-justice Millennial whatever, there is no excuse for men to not have a thorough understanding of the nuances of consent. Today more than ever we should hold men accountable for their actions, and to a high sexual standard. But as women, we infantilize ourselves when we don't take responsibility for our own actions in the bedroom. We have to be able to assess the difference between assault and discomfort. Of course, I'm not saying that if you're a legitimate victim of sexual abuse you should just "get over it." (It feels relevant to note that, often, people who are sexually abused call themselves "survivors" rather than "victims," in an effort to move away from the idea of the passive female victim who's there for the taking.) But we decide what moments in our lives we give power to. We write our own stories. We can decide to define ourselves by our worst experiences—to become victims rather than survivors—or instead, after something bad happens, we can learn from it and move forward. Because realistically, being a fragile victim is just not on-brand for the modern slut.

If I want to reap the benefits of slutdom, I have to have a thick skin. If I want sexual freedom, I have to be able to say no. Slut power is about freedom, but it's also about taking responsibility. The world is not a safe space. There is no such thing as safe sex. We are not victims, we are predators.

cum to the dark side

For decades, feminists have been divided over what should become of the word "slut." There are essentially two camps. The first camp believes that we should eradicate use of the word altogether, arguing that when women call each other sluts—even when it's in an lol feminist bonding way—we're perpetuating slut-shaming and so-called rape culture. It's like when Tina Fey's character in *Mean Girls* tells the group of high schoolers: "You all have got to stop calling each other sluts and whores. It just makes it okay for guys to call you sluts and whores." While *Mean Girls* is basically my bible (I clearly can't go three pages without referencing it), I don't agree with that sentiment. I'm part of camp two, which posits that rather than rejecting the word, we should reclaim it. Historically, many pejorative words have been reclaimed—from "queer" to "butch" to "fag" to "bitch"—by the communities that experienced oppression under those labels. So why should "slut" be any different? It's naive to think that we can simply abolish a word from the social lexicon because it's "mean." (And why would anyone want to get rid of such a wonderfully depraved word, anyway?) Instead, we should take ownership of the slut label, and subvert its negative connotations. Reclaiming a word gives it less ability to harm, and increases its power for provocation and solidarity.

The great feminist slut divide began back in the early nineties, when the Riot Grrrl feminist punk rock movement became the first group to attempt to reclaim the word. I was in my early twenties when I discovered the Riot Grrrl band Bikini Kill, and I remember vividly the first time I saw that iconic photo of singer Kathleen Hanna with "slut" scrawled across her stomach in red lipstick. She looked so impossibly cool. And not only was her message immediately effective, it was also just really funny. Like, girl didn't give a *fuck*. In that moment, I realized that it was possible to hijack a word intended to hurt you, and reappropriate it as an instrument of power and irreverence.

I felt similarly the first time I saw a video of Annie Sprinkle's performance art piece *Public Cervix Announcement*. In the performance, Sprinkle—the legendary artist, porn star, academic, and sex educator—sat on a chair with her legs spread wide, casually inserted a doctor's speculum into her vagina, and then invited audience members to come look at her cervix with a flashlight. Pretty epic. She did this in more than a dozen countries throughout the nineties, in front of thousands of people, always with a big smile, cracking jokes. When I saw the video, in my early twenties, I was in awe of how playful the whole thing was. Sprinkle—who self-identifies as a "slut goddess"— was radical in her ideas about sexual exploration and slutty acceptance, but her rebellion had so much joy and levity in it. She was the ultimate antivictim. I was like, *Whoa, feminism can be* funny? *Who knew?!*

But not everyone was on the slut train. People in the other camp—the "anti-sluts," if you will—argued that we should reject the word because it illustrates how, historically, women have been categorized based on their sexual relationships with men. They argued that, while embracing the slut persona might be chill and empowering within your enlightened social circle of feminist bloggers and their beta-male entourages, the rest of the world basically doesn't get the joke. So you might think you're being funny, but you're actually perpetuating the sexual double standard. Essentially, this camp believes that in a world where women are hypersexualized, embracing the word "slut" is actually more of a surrender than a radical act of resistance.

That dispute—over whether, by being slutty, we are empowering ourselves or just shooting ourselves in the vagina—has been central to the feminist divide for a long time, but it hit a peak in the early 2000s. As you likely remember, this was the era of *Girls Gone Wild*, striptease workouts at the gym, the "landing strip," and Paris Hilton casually flashing her labia to strangers. In reaction to this, writer Ariel Levy authored *Female Chauvinist Pigs: Women and the Rise of Raunch Culture* (2005). The book was intended as a wake-up call to women, and essentially argued that the hypersexual female culture that's supposedly "empowering" is actually just women taking part in their own objectification. She was basically saying that the freedom to be drunk at da club in Manolos with your vag out wasn't the freedom that Gloria Steinem had in mind.

And that's probably true—the vision of the future painted by the pioneers of feminism likely had more to do with women in higher education than it did with paparazzi pussy shots. But like, why are the two mutually exclusive? Why can't I get a PhD and also jerk off in front of a webcam for money on the weekends? Why can't sluts and nonsluts live together in harmony? Why is it unfathomable that humor and irreverence are valid modes of resistance? At the very least, it sure beats being offended by everything.

While I do think the word "slut" should be reclaimed, I should be clear about what I mean by that. The word "reclaim" is associated with redemption—to reclaim is to recover, to reform, to civilize. That's not exactly what the goal is with "slut," at least in my opinion. We don't want to simply reverse the idea of being a slut from being "bad" to being "good," or from unacceptable to acceptable. There *is* something bad about being a slut—something naughty, controversial, and unpredictable—and I don't think we should lose that. Men don't have to be good, so why should women? The idea that female sexuality is entirely righteous, or that we have a better handle on controlling our sexuality than men, is a great societal delusion (and one that is sometimes perpetuated by feminism). To totally flip the meaning of "slut" into something that's solely positive or empowering denies the darkness that's inherent in slutdom, which is part of what makes it so sexy.

Of course, we want to move toward a society where women aren't slut-shamed and can express themselves without fear. But I think it's possible to cultivate a society that permits healthy sexual exploration, while also maintaining the taboo and transgressive elements of slut life. Like, my goal isn't to be good or normal or accepted. My goal is to be free. (And maybe also to troll society a bit in the process, for good measure).

I've been writing and ranting about sex and relationships for more than a decade, and have never been good at sitting on the sidelines, observing the action from an objective distance. I prefer to dive into a world headfirst, to chronicle my experiences from the inside. This book is no different. *Slutever* is a first-person account of a modern, young(ish) woman navigating sex, love, casual hookups, open relationships, boyfriends, girlfriends, bisexuality, BDSM, breakups, sex work, sex parties, and a whole lot of other slutty stuff, as told from the front lines. This is not a self-help or a how-to situation—*god no*, I wouldn't put you through that. This is more of a call to arms, a confessional memoir, a slut manifesto, as told by a hedonistic, sex-radical libertarian slut in a pink PVC minidress. This is a story of a slut who lives happily ever after—or at least one who doesn't get eaten by zombies.

madonna the whore
chapter I

sex education

What *I'm about to say* is so predictable that it verges on cliché: I grew up in a conservative Catholic family. Yes, I am a slutty Catholic girl. How unoriginal.

I can't say for certain that my parents' insistence on me not having sex directly resulted in me wanting to have sex with everyone all the time forever, but I like to think that it did. Of course, there is no single defining truth. There are a million defining truths. But since I'm the one telling this story, I control the narrative. And in my version, growing up Catholic made me a slut. And spending every Sunday in church, gazing up at a giant stained-glass image of the stations of the cross—which, let's be real, is straight BDSM—directly resulted in me becoming a dominatrix. And I'll definitely credit the Madonna-whore complex for my later foray into sex work. It all fits together so nicely.

Today, I relish knowing that two of my sex-radical heroes—those being none other than pop icon Madonna and the controversial pro-sex feminist Camille Paglia—

grew up in devout Catholic, Italian American families, just like myself. A coincidence? Probably not. When I think of growing up Catholic, I'm always reminded of a quote from Paglia, in an essay she wrote about Madonna in 1990: "Madonna's provocations were smolderingly sexy because she had a good Catholic girl's keen sense of transgression. Subversion requires limits to violate." In other words, nothing is sexier than being told *no*.

Some of my earliest memories are of my mother talking to Jesus. This wasn't exactly standard praying; this was more of a casual conversation. Like, "So, Jesus, should I make chicken or pasta for dinner tonight?" Ya know, just shooting the shit. At one point, she was regularly suggesting to the son of God that Elisabeth Hasselbeck should win *Survivor*. She loved giving J-dog her unsolicited advice.

Neither my dad nor my brother and I ever joined in on her divine monologues, but we'd listen, and it felt like we were somehow included, sort of like our family had its own imaginary friend with whom only my mother could liaise. The only time it bugged me was when I had friends over—the presence of a neutral party always seemed to recontextualize her Jesus convos from being cute and kooky to straight-up batshit. "*Mom*," I'd whine. "Me and Sarah are trying to watch *The Real World*. Go talk to Jesus in your room!"

"This is my house," she'd hit back. "I'll talk to Jesus wherever I want."

"Well, I'm sure Jesus is busy!" I'd shout. "Maybe you should try playing hard to get."

I grew up in a small town in upstate New York—so small that it's technically not even a town but a hamlet. This is where both of my parents were born and raised, and after meeting and falling in love in high school, they married and raised me and my little brother there. To give you a mental picture, it's the sort of place where deer cause traffic jams and people think evolution is a movie starring David Duchovny. It's pretty much your average apple-farming town located on the Hudson River, and while it's undoubtedly beautiful, for a kid it's pretty boring, because nothing ever "happens" there. When I was in high school, for fun my friends and I would hang out in the parking lot of the local grocery store, listening to Britney Spears CDs on repeat (or Green Day if we were feeling alt). On weekends there would usually be a keg party in one of the town's sprawling apple orchards, and we'd get wasted on warm beer and cough syrup and have sex in pickup trucks. That was pretty much the extent of my cultural experience until the age of eighteen. The town has changed quite a lot since I was little—now there's some city overspill, and a few new restaurants that serve craft beer and artisanal whatever, but when I was growing up it was almost exclusively second- and third-generation Italian Catholics, and there were only a handful of places to eat, all of which had names like Tony's and Sal's and played exclusively Frank Sinatra.

My mother worked part-time as a receptionist at a dentist's office, and spent her free time volunteering as a religious educator and watching the Eternal Word Television

Network (aka "the God Channel"). When my dad wasn't working long hours at his office job or screaming at the TV, he devoted his time to the Knights of Columbus, an all-male church organization that I've recently realized might actually be a cult. They would do things like run the beer tent at the town bazaar, host spaghetti fundraisers for people whose houses had been crushed by falling trees, and a variety of other top-secret Jesus stuff that my dad never talked to us about. Besides God and football, my dad's greatest passion was saving money. I have an early memory of him teaching me how to wipe my butt, and explaining that "Using any more than three sheets of toilet paper is a waste of money."

Though our family was never poor—we were the middlest of middle class—my dad refused to spend extravagantly on anything, for any reason. Every summer, when my friends' families went off to Mexico or Europe on vacation, my family went to New Jersey. New Jersey, every year, without fail, from before I can remember all the way until after I graduated high school. To be fair, I did always enjoy our Guido family trips to the Jersey Shore, but by the time I reached double digits, I understood on some level that our fried shrimp–centric vacations were missing an element of glamour.

It's no real surprise that I never got the "sex talk." However, there were a few times when I came home from school to find that my mom had taped a show off the God Channel where either a priest or a nun was preaching about the benefits of chastity. She'd then force me to watch it while she sat next to me on the couch, nodding her head in slow motion. Once, in middle school, I had something close to a mental breakdown after she taped Mother Angelica's special on the joy of virginity over the new episode of *Buffy the Vampire Slayer*.

I'm not a scientist, but it seems obvious that when someone is constantly telling you *not* to have sex, it results in you thinking about sex literally every second. Starting in my early teens, sex became my ultimate fascination—what about it, I wondered, was so special as to make it forbidden? It didn't help that, since the age of about ten, I was a low-key masturbation addict. I would spend hours in the bath, my butt pushed all the way to the end of the tub, legs in the air, so as to position my clit right under the flow of the faucet. If my memory serves me well, most of my masturbation fantasies at that time centered around the girls in bikinis who I'd seen in rap music videos (perhaps because that was one of my only sources of erotic material, but also maybe because my vagina was and seemingly always will be a teenage boy). Roughly every fifteen minutes my dad would bang on the bathroom door, asking me what was taking so long and telling me to stop wasting water. Looking back, it creeps me out to think that he likely had somewhat of a clue what was going on in there.

But I'm pretty sure I was a pervert even before I had any idea about sex or masturbation. Case in point: When I was just five years old, I developed a fixation on these twin girls in my kindergarten class, who had just moved to our town from China. They were in the process of learning

English and could barely communicate, which to a bunch of five-year-olds definitely made them seem like "others." Well, for some reason, I started playing out these long, detailed fantasies in my head where I was physically torturing these twins—tying them up, slapping them, making them cry, et cetera. These fantasies weren't explicitly sexual, but I definitely was both entertained and excited by them. This went on for the whole school year. If I wanted to pass the time while on the bus ride to school, or while sitting in church, I'd just close my eyes and think about tormenting the Chinese twins. It progressed to the point where if I had the chance to kick one of them under the table in class while no one was looking, I would. And they couldn't even tell on me, because they couldn't speak English. It was the perfect crime. Although I *did* get in trouble more than once for opening the door while one of them was in the bathroom, even though the red "stop" sign was clearly visible. At the time I had no context for these twisted daydreams, but I did understand on some level that they were strange, and not something I should casually talk about during playground gossip. But looking back on it years later, I'm like... *Wait, was that a sex thing?*

At the age of thirteen, I made a formal pledge to my mother and grandmother that I would wait until I was married to have sex. In exchange for this ultimately empty vow, I was given a promise ring by my grandmother—fourteen-karat gold, containing a tiny diamond—which was my most prized possession until I lost it while swimming in a lake (which coincidentally happened not too long after I was railed for the first time, which I of course interpreted as a punishment from God). At the time that I made the promise, I truly believed it. I was a big Jessica Simpson fan back then, and since she was so avid about waiting until marriage, I figured that I might as well at least try. Plus, both my mother and grandmother had made it very clear to me that if a woman chose to have sex before marriage, she would spiral out of control and become a homeless crack-addict spinster who no man would ever dream of marrying, or something along those lines.

Suffice to say, the Madonna-whore complex was instilled in me from a young age. The term "Madonna-whore complex" was first coined by Sigmund Freud—aka the father of psychoanalysis, who most women today look back on with an eye-roll emoji—and describes a dichotomy in which men view women as either saintly, virginal Madonnas, or sexual, skanky "whores." Freud believed this complex emerged in men because of developmental disabilities, but others attribute it to the way in which women are represented in mythology and Judeo-Christian theology. And as someone who was forced to read the Bible cover-to-cover in my tweens, I can vouch for the fact that biblical women are either undefiled, bride-worthy maidens or thirsty skanks. And since I had no interest in becoming persona non grata to the entire male population at just thirteen, my vague game plan was just to date the bathroom faucet until I met "the one," and then let him unwrap me like the gift that I was on our wedding night.

Yeaaah, that didn't pan out. I lost my virginity at sixteen, to my boyfriend of a week. He was in the grade below me, and was freakishly tall and scrawny, with these big Dumbo ears and an Adrien Brody nose. Shoulder-length brown hair, sunken eyes, freckles. His nickname, in a coup de force of imagination, was Bones. He was so beautiful, I could puke. I'm pretty sure the way he looked informed my "type" for the rest of my life, because almost everyone I've dated since then looks like some version of an insectile human line drawing. (After the first time I introduced Bones to my mom, she scolded, "Karley, I've seen him with his mother at the grocery store. I thought he was a special needs child.") I liked that when I hugged him I could wrap my arms all the way around his chest and almost back again—I can't explain why, but it just felt comforting, like how I imagine a wrestler feels when his opponent enters the ring and he realizes he's got a solid thirty pounds on the guy.

Bones and I boned in the woods behind the football field one day after school. (It really doesn't get more teen-movie than that.) It lasted about thirty seconds. We hadn't even gotten all of our clothes off before Bones came into his baggy blue condom. It didn't even hurt like everybody said it would—probably because I'd been casually sticking shampoo bottles up there for multiple years at this point—but it didn't feel good, either. It just kind of…was. But I wasn't bothered about the whole pleasure aspect of sex at this point. It's sort of like when you first start drinking alcohol—you're not concerned with the taste or quality, or any of the subtle or ostensibly so-phisticated pleasures of drinking. You're just trying to get *fucked*. Well, that's how I felt about sex.

After the anticlimactic football field encounter, I didn't feel as though I'd learned what sex was like—rather, I felt like I'd learned what sex was like *with Bones*. Now the quest became to discover what sex was like with, ya know…everyone else. As you can imagine, my parents were really strict, which threw a bit of a wrench in my newfound teen-ho aspirations. I always had the earliest curfew of all my friends. Once, when I asked if I could go to a high school baseball game, my dad responded, "Are you kidding? I know what happens at baseball games. I'm not paying for an abortion." Since my parents didn't let me have boys over to the house, I had to get experimen-tal with finding alone time with guys. This meant that my high school years involved a lot of sex in cars, on base-ball fields after dark, in parking lots—all very classy. The sex, of course, was terrible—but so fun. At the time I was into younger guys, and when you're sixteen and fucking guys younger than you, they tend to be virgins (and conve-niently desperate). By the end of my high school career, I'd taken six virginities. I was and am still too proud of this.

During those early slutty adventures, there was a part of me that I suppose felt something close to guilt. I under-stood that what I was doing was "bad"—at least, accord-ing to everyone around me, my church, and most of what I'd seen on TV. But it felt thrilling to be bad. It's basic psychology: It's fun to do bad things (I think the young meme prophet Latarian Milton said that). And with all that shame and sin and suppression, we Catholics have *a lot* to work with. To quote John Waters, "I thank God I was raised Catholic, so sex will always be dirty."

After I entered into what I like to call my "teen sex-mania phase" (also known as junior year), on multiple occasions, close friends of mine sat me down for *Dawson's Creek*–style "We're worried about you" conversations. Apparently having more sexual partners than you can count on one hand by eleventh grade warranted an intervention. At school there was a never-ending rumor that I had "the clap"—though no one seemed to have a firm understanding of what the clap actually was. At first I just brushed it off. *They're jealous*, I told myself. But it was difficult not having friends who I could confide in about these experiences. (Remember, this was early internet days, so I couldn't just go to LonelySlutsAnonymous.org or whatever and instantly find a crew of like-minded aspiring deviants; you younger Millennials have it so easy.) There seemed to be an invisible line between talking and thinking about sex, and actually having it. I didn't understand why it was okay for my friends and me to sit around reading *Cosmo* sex tips together, which we did religiously (thanks to *Cosmo*, we all grew up thinking that every relationship problem could be fixed by giving your boyfriend a boob massage), yet when I'd say, "I blew Scott in the shed where they keep the life jackets at the reservoir," my friends would be like, "There's a high chance you have AIDS." There was definitely a dissonance there.

But to be fair, that was on trend at the time. Remember, I was in high school when Britney Spears was writhing around on the floor with a snake singing, "I'm a slave for you," while simultaneously saying that she was waiting until marriage to have sex. It was the *Sex and the City* era, but a few miles north of Samantha, the parents in my town were petitioning to prevent the health department teaching us how to put a condom on a banana. It was a confusing time to be a slut in training.

During the summer before senior year, after I got caught spending the night with a twenty-nine-year-old apple farmer, my parents sent me to a Catholic therapist. Predictably, the therapist tried to further convince me that my sexual behavior was problematic. She said that I used "sex as a weapon" against my family, and against myself. In my rebellious teenage mind, however, I thought the concept of sex-as-weapon sounded really cool, like the ability of a sexual superhero or something. Like my vagina had a machine gun. It could be worse, I thought.

But I wasn't totally immune to the critique. I (unfortunately) am not a sociopath, and after a while, some of the slut-shaming started to get to me. For instance, on the night of the junior prom, one of the most popular boys in my grade brought a blow-up sex doll to the afterparty and wrote my name on its forehead. For the rest of the evening all the jock football bros passed around the doll and mimed having sex with it, finding no end of amusement in this. I was like, *Wow, I do have a gang-bang fantasy, but this is not how I envisioned it would play out.*

In hindsight, so much of this early mockery and social monitoring seems pretty trivial. I also acknowledge that I was objectively "popular," and had life a lot easier than many kids at my school, for instance the girl everyone called Shrek (although to be fair, it was an accurate representation of her). But when you're sixteen, it's hard to imagine a world bigger than high school. You have this idea that what's said about you in the rumor mill—be it good or bad, true or fictionalized, or somewhere in between—is somehow etched into your future identity, and that you will never meet another person who doesn't have a PhD in everything you've ever done and that's been said about you. It can be quite paralyzing.

There was one particularly dark moment that became a kind of turning point for me. It was senior year, and one of my best friends, Courtney, was having a house party while her parents were out of town. We all got zombie wasted—as you do when you're seventeen and still working out that nine vodka shots in an hour might be too many—and in my drunkenness, I ended up banging Courtney's older brother. He was a couple of grades ahead of us in school, and was home visiting from college. I didn't think it would be that big of a deal (slash I didn't think at all), but when word spread through the party that I had disappeared into his bedroom, Courtney went into full-on *Real Housewives* mode. To make a long story short, she barged into his room, grabbed my dress and shoes from his floor, and promptly marched outside and threw them into a bush. I then had to run outside to get my clothes wrapped in just a towel, while the rest of the party looked on, half laughing, half horrified. As I was clawing my way through the shrubbery, searching for my Payless chunky platforms, Courtney and my other closest friends stood watching me from the sidelines, united in bitchface. The night ended with Courtney literally spitting at me in the middle of her driveway, in front of a crowd of like thirty people. For a week afterward, none of my friends would talk to me in school. I felt like I was starring in a teen movie version of *The Scarlet Letter*, except instead of a scarlet *A*, I donned a more early-2000s symbol of shame: a Victoria's Secret thong poking out of my super low-rise jeans, obviously.

To this day I still don't understand what the big deal was. Apparently people don't like it when you fuck their family members? It was like that episode of *Sex and the City* where Charlotte and Samantha have a major falling-out after Samantha fucks Charlotte's brother. For the record, everyone is invited to fuck my family members, as long as you're polite about it. But what I learned from the brother-banging incident—and all the smaller incidents leading up to it—was that being a girl who's casual about her slutca-pades does not sit well with most people. In fact, it often inspires rage. After that, I decided it was probably better to keep my sexual exploits on the DL. And thus spawned my double life—the Clark Kent me that I presented to the world, and the real, slutty superhero me that only came out at night (and sometimes during lunch hour).

By the time I finished high school, in 2004, Clark Kent

me was killing it. I graduated seventh in my class, was an editor of the senior class yearbook, captained both the varsity soccer and basketball teams, played the lead in the school play (*Gentlemen Prefer Blondes*, naturally), was a senior prom queen nominee (still haven't recovered from the loss), and was just generally an all-around star student, friend, daughter, and athlete, with an undoubtedly irritating level of enthusiasm for all of the above. I even made it through most of my final school year without inciting a single sexual intervention from my friends or family members. Yet, leading up to graduation, the conversations with my parents about my college plans never went down so well. My dad was *really* pushing for me to go to West Point, the United States Military Academy, where the students are officers-in-training (or "cadets"), where boot camp is required before entry, and where the tuition is fully funded by the army in exchange for an active duty service obligation upon graduation. *Right.* Despite repeatedly telling my dad that I wanted to be a Hollywood actress and not a soldier, *hello*, I still was forced to visit the West Point campus. "Dad, *as if* I'm gonna go to a college that requires me to wear fatigues," I whined, stomping my Uggs in protest.

Stronger than my aversion to wide-leg camouflage pants, however, was my desire to just *get out*—to remove myself from the busybody social monitoring that anyone who grew up in a small town is all too familiar with. This reminds me: A few years ago, I was listening to Dan Savage's sex advice podcast, *Savage Love*. One of the callers was a teenage boy from somewhere in the Bible Belt, and his question to Savage was essentially this: I just graduated from high school, I've come out as gay, and it's not sitting well with my friends and family. What can I do to make people in my town accept me? Basically: How can I make my life better? And Savage's answer was one that I didn't expect. I expected him to talk about self-acceptance, and therapy, and secret gay mating call hand signals or something. But instead, his answer was: Get on a bus and move to San Francisco. Or Seattle. Or literally anywhere with a vibrant gay community. His point was that while it's nice to hope that one day the world will be more accepting and we'll all be able to channel our inner freak snowflakes or whatever, in the meantime you have to live with the reality that most people in your town just think you're a weird fag. A harsh response, for sure, but I appreciated that.

And I think you can apply that to slutdom, too. Like, there are some people in the world who are just never going to accept or respect a person—particularly a woman—who has a lot of sex, or who just talks openly about sex, and it can be a waste of energy to even try to change their minds. But I mean, whatever, not everyone has to like you, right? (In fact, if everyone did like you, it would mean that you were worryingly inoffensive, aka boring.) Listening to Dan Savage made me so happy that I left home at eighteen, even though I didn't understand the enormity of my decision until later on. It was as if, like my mother had always told me, I truly had a guardian angel on my shoulder, watching out for me. Except my guardian angel just happened to be one of the biblical whores, whispering into my ear: *Go forth, young slut. Find your people.*

sluts who dumpster-dive

Unsurprisingly, my parents were both horrified and confused when, instead of opting for target practice or entering a mediocre state school to study the complex art known as "communications," I moved to London just weeks after finishing high school. I ostensibly went there to study theater, and was enrolled as a drama major at a university in London. But I also just liked the idea of putting an ocean between me and my parents. And so I applied for a passport, got on a plane, and left the country for the first time, on a delusional mission to become a successful playwright and thespian. Things didn't exactly go as planned. You know that cliché: the more overprotective the parents, the more likely the kid is to treat college like a binge-drinking, amateur gang-bang bacchanalia? Well, that was basically my experience. Minus the college part.

It's hard for me to recall the exact headspace I was in when I moved away. But what I do know is that, up until that point, I'd been a person who really cared. I always got good grades, always did the extra credit, was never late to practice, and I tried, for the most part, to seem like a respectable human being. And then suddenly, I just couldn't care anymore. I started partying every day, skipped almost all my classes, slept around (uncircumcised dicks—a new discovery!) and ended up dropping out of college after just one semester. But I liked London, and wanted to stay. Or at least, I didn't want to go home.

Like everyone does, growing up, I'd often imagined my future. There were a number of things that I thought I might grow up to be. An actress was my first choice, but I also thought I might be a news reporter, like Diane Sawyer, with her perfect blond blow-out and crisp Oxford shirts. I briefly entertained the idea of being a lawyer, because I loved *Ally McBeal*. I even, for a while, considered paleontology, on the sole basis that I frequently jerked off thinking about Jeff Goldblum in *Jurassic Park* (who, I worked out later, didn't even play a paleontologist in that movie). Never once, however, did I envision myself growing up to be a vaguely ketamine-addicted degenerate squat rat who ate out of the garbage. Life is funny like that.

When you're an unemployed eighteen-year-old five thousand miles from home with no money, prospects, or responsibilities, you end up in some unique situations. One night, I found myself high on ecstasy, on a party boat in the Thames River. I was dating a guy I'd met at university—a sexy, freckled musician named Sam, whose band was serenading the seasick partygoers, and I'd tagged along for the ride. This is where I serendipitously met Matthew, an artist in his early twenties whose soul I instantly connected with on a profoundly drug-induced level. Matthew stuck out like a sore thumb—he was six foot three, but more like six foot six if you counted his hair, which was a flat-top of brown curls that shot straight out of his head as if he'd just been electrocuted. He was wearing dark eyeliner, lipstick, and a tattered cape, and looked like some sort of urban shaman-slash-goth drag queen. He told me he was squatting in an abandoned elevator factory in south London with a group of nine other artists, musicians, and writers. Squatting, he informed me, was the act of occupying a building that you don't own. So basically you find an empty building, move in, change the locks, and then just stay there rent free until the owner decides he wants you out and takes you to court. "You should totally come visit," Matthew said excitedly. "We make these giant feasts out of food that we find in the bin!" If I had been even 1 percent less high I probably would have passed, but in the moment it sounded very exotic. Or at the very least, not touristy.

The following week, I went over to the squat for what Matthew referred to as a "bin banquet." The rule of the meal was that you couldn't pay for anything. This meant salvaging recently out-of-date packaged food discarded by supermarkets, getting salt and pepper sachets from McDonald's, and stealing bottles of alcohol. That night, Matthew and his arty squat crew made a five-course meal that fed fifteen people, in their thirty-thousand-square-foot warehouse. It was a perfect art-school avant-garde fantasy: acoustic guitars, flower crowns, people rolling filterless cigarettes, people quoting Nietzsche unironically. I think there might have even been a drum circle. Looking back, I understand that, if I had grown up poor, without basic comforts, the idea of eating out of the garbage might have felt less romantic. But I was totally smitten. While the term "squad goals" hadn't yet hit the zeitgeist back in 2005, I knew instantly, on that first night, that I desperately wanted to be one of their crew.

At this point in my life, I was just sort of floating. Ever since dropping out of university I had been low-key homeless, spending most nights at Sam's or squeezing uninvited into his band's crappy minibus as they toured around the country playing mostly empty dive bars. I was essentially being a professional girlfriend, and was beginning to feel like I needed my own life. So when Matthew suggested I should move in with him, I jumped at the offer. (To clarify, Matthew is gay, and thus is a rare character in this story in that we were not boning.) However, moving in wasn't that simple. See, the squat functioned as a commune, and members shared everything from food to clothing, and adding a new person into the mix meant further splitting the bounty. In order to regulate the number of occupants, each time someone wanted to invite someone new into the house, all the existing squatmates had to vote on whether to accept or reject the applicant. It was essentially like applying to live in one of those Upper East Side co-ops, except the super-gross version.

In order to prove myself worthy to the squat board, I spent a couple of weeks crashing in Matthew's bed, doing daily dumpster raids to show that I was a competent scavenger, and stealing cheap vodka from Lidl to prove my adeptness in petty thievery. I ripped holes in my tights, smudged my eyeliner, and stopped brushing my teeth, hoping to fit in. In the final vote, I was narrowly accepted. The people who didn't want me to move in (I never found out exactly who), Matthew explained, were mainly worried that the building was just getting too crowded. There was only one bathroom, which meant eleven people sharing one toilet and one electric shower (there was no hot water in the building, but they'd installed an electric heater in the shower, which was powerful enough to produce lukewarm water for about three minutes once every hour). Plus, all the rooms were occupied. This meant I had the choice of either sleeping on a couch in the "living room"—a huge, open warehouse space, which clearly provided no privacy—or living in the stairwell. I chose the stairwell.

You know those really big factory stairwells that have a landing halfway up the story? Well, that landing was my bedroom. It was just large enough to fit a full-size mattress, with about a foot of space left over on one side. The staircase led from the second floor up to the roof, which luckily meant it was rarely used. I used the steps as shelves for my clothes. I hung posters of Louis Garrel and *Billy Elliot* on the walls. I bought a blue lightbulb. It actually ended up looking pretty cool. I mean, there were obvious downsides. For example, the cement walls and the high ceilings made heating the space nearly impossible, so during the winter it was freezing. Once, after sex, I watched Sam pull off his condom, and you could literally see steam rising off his cock, it was so cold. While my new, superficially bleak living situation clearly took a bit of getting used to, it wasn't long before that small, dark, cold, mold-scented cement platform felt alarmingly like home.

Before I moved to London, I'd never had a gay friend or an artist friend. My idea of "alternative culture" was anyone who wore Converse. My idea of gay culture was *Will & Grace*, and my knowledge of art was limited to the watercolor landscapes of the Jersey Shore they sold at the local craft fair, which always ended up in our bathroom. Unfortunately, not all of us can be Gaby Hoffmann, growing up in the Chelsea Hotel with a Warhol Superstar for a mother, or Lena Dunham, honing her craft for oversharing among art world glitterati in a trendy Tribeca loft. After moving to London, sometimes I literally felt like I had grown up in a black hole. Like the time someone in the school cafeteria had to explain to me what sushi was. Or the time Sam told me he was in an indie band, and I thought that meant he was from India. Like, I was straight up *basic*. I had chunky Kelly Clarkson highlights. I wore spaghetti-strap tank tops. I had that awkward type of crunchy hair that never looks fully dry. I felt at home in a tanning bed. And then suddenly I'm living in an elevator factory with an Iranian asylum seeker, a Russian goth stylist, a woman who said the word "aura" like ten times a day, a performance artist who puked milk rainbows, and a bunch of other freaks, most of whom looked at me like *I* was the weirdo.

For the first time in my life, I would wake up every morning feeling excited and just completely in awe of the people and things around me. It was amazing how much life these people were living on essentially no money. I was dirt poor, but I somehow never seemed to notice. No one had anything, so everything was everyone's. At one point I worked behind the bar at a pub for a few months, making £4.40 an hour, until I realized that it was literally possible to find more money on the ground at nightclubs than I made at my job, so I quit. Matthew and I would go out every night and get drunk on Lidl vodka that tasted like battery acid. We threw massive raves in our basement and built giant art installations to party in. Once, we built a giant papier-mâché vagina that you could crawl through to get to the "chill-out womb," and if you wanted some privacy you could plug the entrance with a giant bloody tampon we made out of painted Styrofoam (hashtag period art, hashtag feminism). Our refrigerator was always overflowing with food (out of date, but still). There were always so many people around that you never got lonely. It felt opulent, somehow. "Penniless decadence" is what Matthew called it. The penniless part is pretty self-explanatory, but the decadence of it was multilayered—it was the leisure, and the lack of responsibility; it was the decaying grandeur of living in a derelict building; it was the irony of being totally broke but having a five-thousand-square-foot living room. There was nothing I wanted that I didn't have. While it's impossible to quantify these sorts of things, it's clear to me now that this period of my life was fundamental in shaping who I am, in ways that are probably more extreme than I could ever imagine.

Being around Matthew also made me feel confident, like anything was possible. He made me feel like I could wear clothes that I picked up off the street, and as long as I had the right attitude, I would look cool. I was pretty chubby during that time—despite not actually being in college, I still gained the freshman fifteen, plus another fifteen for good measure. It was like my body intuitively knew that I was living in a cement warehouse with no heating, and it was preparing itself for winter by compelling me to eat street hot dogs at 2 a.m. every night. But by some miracle, I didn't care about my weight. In high school, less than a year earlier, I'd cared *so* much about the way I looked. I was pretty much your average teen girl: I dabbled in anorexia for a while but ultimately quit when I could no longer explain why I kept fainting at basketball practice. Then I gave bulimia a test drive, but all the puking was causing these gross broken blood vessels to pop up all over my face. After my bulimia fail, I resigned to counting calories and just sort of casually hating myself, which was pretty much my MO up until I started squatting. But suddenly, after meeting Matthew and Co., I was heavier than I'd ever been, and I didn't care. It was almost like I was too happy to even realize that I had put on weight. I also suddenly no longer cared about looking "pretty." On a whim, I ditched my chunky highlights and shaved half my head, dyed my remaining hair neon blue, and let Matthew use a Sharpie to temporarily tattoo leopard print onto my naked skull. My uniform was a pair of dirt-caked Doc Martens, a ripped nightie, smudged makeup, and too much cleavage. I looked like an apocalyptic garbage whore and smelled like a combination of vodka and semen, but I felt great about myself. I remember once Matthew said something that really stuck with me. He said, "I don't want to look hot so that people want to fuck me. I want to look powerful so that people believe in me. I want people to see me and think, 'That person is free.'" And sure, it sounds sort of naive, but there's a sentiment there that I still really respect.

It won't surprise you that one of my biggest style inspirations was Courtney Love. At the time I didn't know much about her, beyond her being the singer of Hole and Kurt Cobain's baby mama, but I was intuitively drawn to her aesthetic and the tough, slutty, girly-girl attitude it projected. As has happened at multiple points throughout my life, I wasn't aware of the political or feminist connotations of that style choice until way later. In her essay "Sluts and Riot Grrrls: Female Identity and Sexual Agency" (*Journal of Gender Studies*, 2007), Feona Attwood unpacks the politics of Courtney Love's iconic style. She outlines how Love's look subverts normative depictions and understandings of female sexuality.

> Courtney Love, the most visible performer to be identified with Riot Grrrl, adopted a…"kinder-whore" look, combining very girly, sometimes torn, "babydoll" dresses with heavy and often smudged make-up; "a slutty, D.I.Y. subversion of the traditional Prom queen look."

Kim Nicolini argues that the slut persona as performed by Love involved a rejection of both "Good Girl" and "Good Feminist" roles in order to "take all the mess of female sex and throw it into the public eye." Combining pretty and ugly qualities; the babydoll and the witch, "the glistening sex doll and the screeching life buried under the pink plastic," Love created an "attraction/repulsion dynamic" capable of making audiences question their attitudes towards female sexuality...This kind of performance, embodied by Love, but evident elsewhere in girl subcultures, is a complicated kind of alchemy, on the one hand transforming a position of shame and powerlessness into one of confrontation, yet on the other maintaining a sense of ambivalence and hybridity. The awkwardness of this is particularly evident in performances of the slut persona which often literally signify difficulty by appearing cheap, loud, ugly, noisy, broken, repellent, used and out of control, Other and abject, monstrous and possessed. The "mess" of female and femininity—essence and artifice—appropriates male space and behaviour in loud, angry public appearances. It disturbs the limits of acceptable feminine behaviour and the boundaries of heterosexual style and performance.

The way we dress is, of course, part of how we construct our personal narrative. It's the clearest gesture of our desires, our identity, and how we feel about ourselves at any given time. And maybe dressing like a freak or a slut is just a normal youthful rite of passage, but at that point in my life, dressing like a Courtney Love impersonator felt like strapping on armor. It's like how an actor puts on a costume to help get into character—in my trashed nightie, it was like I suddenly had permission to dance on tables and make out with guys on buses and just generally be an annoying hot mess—but one who was having a lot of fun.

The era of the elevator factory lasted just over a year. But all good things must come to an end—as must all squats. Eventually the owner took us to court, and soon we were on the streets. At this point, the squat crew largely dispersed. Most of them were older than me, and some went on to get real jobs and real houses. Some became homeless, some became famous. I, however, was still professionally figuring out my life, so I decided to join a different squat crew—a younger crew, some of whom I knew because I literally kept running into them inside dumpsters (it's like the equivalent of a social club for freegans). This new squat was far less of a, shall I say, "structured" living arrangement. While the elevator factory had been a sort of avant-garde wannabe-communist wannabe-utopia, the new squat was more like living in a psych ward, if the psych ward was also a drug den where everyone was constantly having sex and giving each other lice.

For the next three years of my life, home was a dilapidated four-story hostel in southeast London. I doubt most sane human beings could inhabit a place so vile. Like in many squats, there was no heating or hot water, but that was the least of our problems. The floors were carpeted with empty beer cans and discarded Pot Noodle containers. Most of the windows were either smashed or covered in graffiti. In the living room, a permanent chandelier of flies hung from the center of the ceiling. There was so much junk in that room that we began stacking new junk on top of the old junk, forming large junk mountains that we had to literally scale in order to maneuver through the space. There was a big couch that sat crookedly atop a small couch, a birdcage big enough to fit a small adult, assorted mannequin body parts (a requirement of any authentic college-age living space), a collection of more than a hundred VHS tapes, and a constant rotation of bodies, most of whom I recognized, many of whom I didn't. The air was thick with the scent of wet cigarettes and dried blood. This is where I spent some of the best years of my life.

There were between ten and fifteen of us who lived in the hostel, depending on the day—a ramshackle crew of drifters, losers, addicts, anarchists, and that special type of artist who never actually produces any art. One of my closest friends in the squat was Claire, a wispy nineteen-year-old ketamine dealer and aspiring prostitute. I kept trying to tell Claire that prostitution is rarely a profession that people *struggle* to break into, yet somehow she spent the six months after I met her trying to become a whore with no success. *How is this possible?* I wondered. The problem wasn't the way she looked. She was really hot— long skyscraper legs, a shiny black bob, and these puffy red lips that always looked freshly sucked on. The problem, rather, was that she was an airhead. See, Claire came from a long line of hippie ravers. Whenever she would tell us a story from her childhood, it would start with something like: "During my first acid trip, when I was seven," or "Back when we lived in a box…" I met her mother twice, and both times she was wearing fairy wings—like, at lunchtime. Claire once told me that it wasn't until she started school and saw the other kids putting milk on their Cheerios that she learned most people don't eat cereal with Coca-Cola. Because of stories like these, the rest of us in the house forgave Claire when she regularly asked us questions like "What's a lobster?" or casually mistook Auschwitz for a shopping mall in Berlin.

There were a handful of other core squatmates. First there was Sebastian, who at twenty-five was the elder of the house. Sebastian had big, protruding teeth that looked like they were at war with each other (like most British people) and played guitar in a vaguely famous indie band (like most British people). Then there was Dirk, the gay kid with dyed green hair, who only wore green and brown clothing, because he wanted to look "like a tree." Next was Rabbit, the lanky, Canadian bisexual who was obsessed with conducting satanic masturbation rituals using (supposedly) magical symbols knows as "sigils." So basically he'd casually ask Satan for something he wanted, and then draw some squiggly lines onto a piece of paper and jerk-off onto it. After Rabbit moved in, it became commonplace to find a group of people masturbating in a circle in the living room, backed by a soundtrack of Peruvian flute music. Next was Sofía, the boy-crazy Colombian who dressed like every day was Coachella. I can't forget Bea, the impressively flexible teenage ecstasy addict. And Dan, the bearded political cartoonist who never showered and whose dick gave me a perma–yeast infection. Kat, the argumentative Scottish anarchist, and her girlfriend Laura, an American synth musician who wore a skeleton costume pretty much every day. Dylan, a gay jewelry designer with a PhD in convincing straight boys to experiment with their sexuality. And last but not least, there were "the Czechs," a group of Eastern European bike messenger graffiti stoner bros who lived in the hostel's windowless basement. I'm not sure if *all* of them were actually from the Czech Republic, but one of them said he was at some point, and then the name just sort of stuck. The number of Czechs was always changing, but in general most of them had dreads, couldn't speak English, and were on a constant rotation in and out of jail. It was a beautifully deranged little family, and I fell in love with them all.

They say that necessity breeds invention. This was more of a "boredom breeds idiocy" situation. As you might imagine would happen when you put a dozen unemployed twenty-one-year-olds into a minimansion, the hostel became a breeding ground for the absurd. One of my favorite squat memories is of the time Claire came up with a genius plan for how to keep the house clean with minimal effort. The answer was simple, she told us: We should get a slave. Obviously.

When she suggested this, all of us brushed it off, assuming it was just one of her brain malfunctions. But Claire insisted that, by the magic of the internet, she had found us a slave who was willing to clean up after us in exchange for the small price of being emotionally and physically abused. It sounded too good to be true.

Claire had happened upon the aspiring slave's ad on Gumtree.com (the British version of craigslist) and decided to go and talk with the guy, bringing along Kat as moral support, aka security. They went to meet the slave at a local café—both wearing stolen thrift store blazers, on Claire's insistence that it was a "business meeting"— to discuss how things would go down. While I can't imagine that interviewing for the position of someone's unpaid servant is a very rigorous process, the dude apparently passed with flying colors, and a few days later our very own slave showed up on our doorstep.

The slave was an Asian guy in his thirties who worked as a lawyer when he wasn't cleaning strangers' toilet bowls for sexual pleasure. At first it was amazing. He would come and clean for us once a week, and we didn't have to pay him a dime. He'd just cheerfully scrub the floors while we lay around watching reruns of *America's Next Top Model*, and every once in a while one of us would get up and whip him with a phone charger. We felt like we'd uncovered this incredible secret, like "Wait…why don't *more* people have slaves? It's such an efficient way of getting things done!"

At first, some of the people in the house didn't realize

that the slave didn't actually live with us. At one point, while we were indulging in our Saturday afternoon ritual of drinking White Russians and playing charades, Dirk looked confused when the man came into the living room with a broom and dustpan.

"Why are you *cleaning*?!" Dirk yelled, horrified, as if the guy had just pointed a machine gun at us.

"No, no—that's our slave," Claire whispered, after which Dirk looked puzzled for a second, but then just shrugged it off, like *I'm not even going to bother to ask.*

At this point, I was still a BDSM novice. All of us in the house were. What we didn't realize at the time, being newbies in the world of kink, was that while slaves don't want to be paid money, they do want to be paid a lot of attention. We assumed that we could just be napping/ unconscious while the dude dusted around us. Not so. Turns out, the turn-on isn't cleaning; the turn on is being *watched* while cleaning. After a few weeks of coming over, the slave started giving *us* performance reviews, claiming that we were not engaged enough as proprietors. Naturally, we were outraged. This wasn't the power dynamic we'd signed up for. But we didn't want to lose him—I mean, the house looked better than ever, and we had come to appreciate the simple joy of not living in a literal pile of trash—so we decided to make more of an effort. Rather than just hitting the slave with random things we found on the floor, Claire stole some whips from a sex shop. I put on a leather skirt. Sebastian cut a hole in a garbage bag (the poor man's latex) and wore it like a dress. We also got more involved in the slave's creative process by making a specific list of tasks for him to accomplish. I recently found a photo of the list in one of my early blog entries. It read as follows:

- De-mold entire house
- paint atlas of world on living room wall
- fix all broken windows (3)
- clean crab terrarium
- alphabetize all VHS tapes
- decorate upstairs bathroom (aquatic theme)
- sew rips on couch (may be impossible)
- clean kitchen (may be impossible)

The slave was kind of an asshole, honestly. For a slave-identifying person, he was pretty full of himself. He started refusing to do certain chores, claiming moral authority over us. For instance, since no one showered, we had turned the bathtub into a terrarium, filled it with rocks and marine plants, and made it the home of our pet crab. As one does. But when Claire told the slave to clean the terrarium, he was all like, "That crab is going to die. You can't only feed it out-of-date sandwiches from Marks and Spencer." And we were like, "Are you a fucking crab rights activist? Mind your own business."

After our first fight, the relationship was never the same again. After just a month of servitude, our slave broke up with us. Apparently, even someone whose ambition in life is to be dehumanized and humiliated couldn't handle how tragic we were.

One of the perks of squatting is that it leaves you with a lot of good stories. It also leaves you a lot of free time to make bad art. So really, I have squatting to blame for starting my blog *Slutever*, which I launched around this time, at twenty-one. This was back in OG blogspot days, in 2007, back before everyone and their dog had a blog, and when people still thought it was a good idea to write in pink comic sans font on a black background.

At the beginning, the blog was mainly just oversharey rants about the debauchery of everyday squat life, posts about my sexual fantasies (there's an early post about finding sharks erotic, which I hope I was lying about), and stories about my sexual exploits from high school. I discovered that writing about my teenage sexual experiences was cathartic and gave me a sense of retroactive power over sexual situations that had at times felt more cursory. And, as an added bonus, people seemed to like to read it. I got my first paid writing jobs because of the blog, mostly through *Vice* (which was also in its early, ranty, offensive stage, so I fit right in).

A problem, however, was that I was still dating Sam at the time. Sam was not so into my new venture of slut blogging. Sam deserves his own chapter (and gets it), but here's some context, from my personal and biased perspective: Sam was a virgin when we met, and when I started writing publicly about stuff like peeing on a twenty-nine-year-old guy during sex when I was sixteen, he felt threatened. He didn't like that I had an array of sexual experiences that predated him. He was also embarrassed that his family, who I was very close to, had discovered the blog and were reading it, too. It didn't help that I then started writing about sex with Sam, particularly about the fact that he had a disability, and how that affected our sex life. I admit that I was really insensitive at the time. It took me years of offending and embarrassing my friends and lovers with things that I wrote about them to finally learn that not everyone wants the intimate details of their life blabbed about on the internet. Whoops. Live and learn, I guess. But the point is, the blog ultimately put the nail in the coffin of my and Sam's four-year relationship. And when we broke up, his parting neg was that, going forward, no dude in his right mind was ever going to date a sex writer.

Of course, being single made my blog way better. It's hard to write a slut blog when you have a boyfriend, honestly. My new single self was primed for a rampage of sexual discovery, and this time, I wouldn't just be fucking around in defiance of my totalitarian parents. This time I could write off my slutty exploits as *research*. There's another John Waters quote that I love, where he says: "Before I was paid to be a writer, people thought I was crazy to just go on these little missions of things that would interest me. But now that I get paid to do it, people say 'Oh, how interesting.' So, I think that's really the difference between being a writer and a crackpot." That pretty much sums up how I felt at the time. I was no longer just a slut. I was a slut with a cause.

The slut gods must have been looking out for me, because just days into my newfound singledom, I found myself locked in a bedroom with Kat and some random French guy. There was a party at the squat, and the three of us had gone into Kat's bedroom to try on the elf costumes that she'd stolen from her new job as a professional elf at the London Dungeon experience, but while trying to leave Kat accidentally yanked the handle off the door. After spending twenty minutes aimlessly stabbing a pen into the hole where the knob had been, we gave up and had a threesome. With a light elf role-play component. I'd never had a threesome before, and was surprised at how playful the vibe was. I had also assumed that all group sex situations required a jealous outburst, or tears, or at the very least a light stabbing. But this was nothing like the murderous love triangles I'd seen in erotic thrillers (though the elf costumes might have played a role in that).

Around hour three of our lock-in we all got really dehydrated. Thankfully, Dylan came to our rescue by tying a water bottle to our cat's neck and forcing it to walk along the narrow ledge between his bedroom window and our temporary jail. At one point the bottle rolled off the end of the ledge and we were pretty certain the cat was going to fall four stories to its death, but it ended up being fine. We were trapped in there for eight hours before a locksmith finally came and freed us. My biggest revelation of the saga was that group sex is amazing for when you're drunk, because you can just take a time-out whenever you're bored or tired and someone else will literally take over for you. Genius.

Weirdly, my parents didn't find this story amusing. In

fact, they weren't really fans of any of my writing. Post-blog, they became more vocal about how horrified they were that I'd bailed on the life that God had planned for me and instead chosen to fall down a K-hole of amorality. Beyond just being worried about me and embarrassed for themselves, they were concerned about the long-term effects that writing about sex would have on my subsequent professional life and ability to trap a husband. Like Sam, my mother was pretty insistent that blogging about being a ho was going to make it difficult to ever find anyone to love me. Her panicked emails to me from that time are pretty classic. Being the bitch that I was, rather than being sympathetic to her quite valid personal crisis, I'd usually just post snippets from her emails on my blog as a joke. And now, because I've yet to mature, I'm going to do it again here. The following are a selection of excerpts from my mother's emails from 2007 to 2009.

> Karley, there are a few things that have been both-ering me lately and I need to get some things off my chest. It bothers me unbelievably that the one thing that you choose to write about is "dirty things." Is that who you really are? Is that because you feel nobody would read your writing if it wasn't all about sex? I know you know it bothers me. I think it's only natural that it would bother me and Dad and anybody who loves you. Can you at least try and understand how it makes me feel?

Karley, I went on the Vice blog today and I am seriously afraid to read your articles sometimes. I feel like whenever I enter that site I see something about vaginas, and I know that's your favorite subject (????) so I don't read the article in fear that you wrote it!

Rob [my little brother] had Facebook open the other day so I took a quick look at your page, and I'm worried about what you say on your "wall." When I looked you had written something about how your vagina had started its own PR company. Is that meant to be funny? I don't understand your humor sometimes.

Let Jesus back into your heart.

This clubnight "Girlcore" that you organize, is it true that this is a lesbian night or is that just for show?

I can't hold my head up in the supermarket anymore because I feel like the whole town is looking at me and judging me because of your blog. Don't you have any respect for how your actions reflect on me and Daddy?

You are twenty three years old. Why is it that you are so "into" a nineteen year old boy who looks twelve? Also, you say that he acts "crazy" and that obviously does not make me feel good. It seems like instead of getting more mature as you age you are acting more crazy and talking about getting drunk and having hangovers all the time. Please set me straight if I'm wrong, but can you see why I am so worried about you?

There has been lots of coverage in the press about HPV recently and it makes me so nervous! Are you making sure to use protection?

I called you three times yesterday and you didn't pick up. Please respond to this email and let me know you're not dead.

Instead of blogging, maybe you should try making a vision board. It's a list of personal goals using visual images. I saw it on Oprah. Just a thought!

They're pretty poetic. It's easy for me to laugh about this stuff today, because I now have a deeply loving relationship with my parents (in part because we eventually agreed to disagree about my writing). But in my early twenties, there were a few years when things were pretty bad between us. After I started my blog, I barely spoke to either of my parents for three years. In my infrequent phone conversations with my mom, a reoccurring theme was the idea that I had "been corrupted"—that I was ultimately a person of virtue but had been led astray, and that the farther away I wandered, the harder it would be for me to find my way back.

"You used to be such a good girl," she'd say repeatedly. Sometimes she'd be crying. While I clearly wasn't going to take her life advice, this still wasn't easy to hear.

"Good girl" is a phrase that often gets used in our culture, whether it's Drake cooing that "you're a good girl and you know it," or our dads repeatedly telling us to "be a good girl" throughout our adolescence. Usually, being a "good girl" means something along the lines of being quiet, polite, and well-behaved, and not sucking strangers' dicks in an alleyway behind a warehouse party. I don't know…sounds kinda boring to me. Of course, what goes hand in hand with the idea of the good girl is the trope of the "good girl gone bad"—this notion that as women, we are naturally sweet and pure and good-hearted, until one fateful day when we eat the forbidden fruit, and then it all goes to shit.

Of course, this is reductive and harmful (and, like, makes no sense). No one is either all good or all bad. We are neither Madonnas nor whores. We don't all start out pure and become "corrupted." Just like men, women are complex human beings, and can't be reduced to this infantilizing polarity. The reality is, being a girl who likes to fuck, who pursues visceral sexual experiences, is neither good nor bad—but it does make life more interesting.

harnessing my slut powers
chapter 2

temporarily insane

"The hole you're trying to fill* is not in your pussy, your ass, or your mouth," Max told me, sometime around the beginning of our relationship. "You need to figure out what's missing in your life and tend to it, otherwise you're just going to end up fucking yourself into oblivion."

Was that an insult, or just really good advice? I couldn't tell. But it didn't matter. Honestly, I loved it when Max spoke to me this way, because it meant that he was analyzing me. Or at least that he was *thinking* about me at times other than when he was inside me. I took this as a sign that we must be soul mates.

I knew from the start that our relationship was a bad idea, but I was okay with that. Truth be told, I found it oddly thrilling to think that my romance with Max could potentially ruin my life. I was twenty-four, had just arrived in New York City, and was falling in what I suppose would be called love. Max—the object of my obsession— was a twenty-three-year-old, Asperger's-esque chemistry student and documentary filmmaker who I'd masturbated to at least forty times before we'd ever actually met. Max was beautiful: six foot one and 113 pounds, like an over-grown dandelion, aka my ideal male body type. When he inhaled, it looked as if his ribs were about to pierce through his skin. His deep-set eyes were like two caves. As I've made quite clear, I melt for that translucent, tuber-culo look.

My relationship with Max began in my head. I was still living in London at the time, and happened to come across one of his documentaries online, in which he trav-eled to the rain forest to be ritualistically burned and dosed with hallucinogenic venom. When I saw him on my laptop screen, I swear I nearly gasped. His shirtless body, which was covered in bug bites and dirt, looked worryingly underinflated. He was the personification of every mental sketch I'd ever created of the "perfect boy." His voice alone made me want to fuck him: warped and uncomfortably deep, like a cassette tape that had been left out in the sun too long. The problem, of course, was that I lived in London and he lived thousands of miles away in New York. Woe was me.

Around this time, I was toying with the idea of the in-ternet as a sort of God figure—if you wanted something, I thought, all you had to do was ask the internet for it and it would be yours. My theory was that, since almost every-one has a Google alert for their name, if you blog about someone enough, they will eventually see it. And if you seem desperate enough, they will eventually fuck you.

This strategy had *sort of* worked for me once before.

A couple of months earlier, I'd written a blog post about my childhood obsession with that sickly wheelchair kid from the movie *The Secret Garden*. He was my first ever crush, which confused my mother, seeing as the character was literally an invalid. In my blog post, I included the name of the actor who played him, who I knew was now twenty-eight and also lived in London (though at this point unfortunately had some color in his cheeks and was sans wheelchair). I wrote about how I slept under a poster of him all throughout my tweens, and how I'd lie in bed at night and imagine what color his pee was (luminous yellow). Ya know, nothing too scary. My Google God premonition was correct, because within days the actor sent me an email, informing me that the color of his pee depended on the amount of fluids he drank, but that it was generally normal colored. Amazing. Unfortunately we never fucked, although we did awkwardly kiss once when I ran into him in the street outside a bar at 2 a.m., which to this day is one of the highlights of my life, because it made me feel that, on some level, I was in control of the universe. Some people pray; I blog.

And so I began writing a series of irrationally obsessive blog posts about my infatuation with Max: how I would set a place setting for him at my dinner table every night and imagine he was there eating with me; how I would make out with my hand in the shower and pretend it was his mouth I was tonguing, and so on. Lo and behold, within a week the internet gods had answered my request in the form of a Facebook message from the Lust of My

Life. It read simply: "I've seen the blogs. Are you ever in New York? If so, we should hang out." I almost puked.

Coincidentally (or not?), six months later I was deported from the UK after being caught coming back into London on the Eurostar with an expired visa. Whoops? And so I moved to New York, because…well, where else is there? Max and I had not kept in contact in the months leading up to this point (aka he never replied to my responding message, which involved asking if I could change my Facebook status to "in a relationship"), but I took my sudden deportation as a sign from the sex gods that he and I were meant to be. All I needed to do now was get his attention. I wanted to do something grand— to make a big impression—and so I creepily found out where he lived through a mutual acquaintance, put on a ten-dollar thrift-store polyester wedding dress I'd bought back in the ninth grade, and sat on the doorstep of his apartment building in ninety-degree heat, waiting for him to come home. Obviously. What felt like hours later, but might have been twenty minutes, I watched as Max's mantis-like body moved toward me in an awkward lurch. As I gazed up at him, my body perspiring profusely under the layers of polyester, he flashed me a look of simultaneous confusion and fear. "I think we may have met in a past life," he said after a long pause. We fucked within thirty minutes.

And so began the start of what I defined as a relationship, but what most people would probably call a tragedy. The problem with Max was that he didn't really like to, ya know, leave his apartment or interact with other human beings or have fun or have sex or be nice to me. It put a bit of a damper on things, honestly. But still, he seemed to like having me around once in a while, and I was just dumbfounded by the fact that I was somewhat regularly IRL-fucking the guy who I'd been masturbating to online for more than a year.

With Max, I suddenly found myself doing cliché "scary girlfriend" things that I'd seen in movies, like secretly smelling his dirty underwear or making myself come while watching him sleep. I was, quite plainly, creepily infatuated with him. Or at least, with the fantasy of him that I'd created in my head.

The problem is, when you're in love with someone and they're indifferent to you, it drives you fucking insane. It seems unlikely that Max was *entirely* apathetic toward me, given that we were dating or whatever, but it did appear that way a lot of the time. I was new to New York, but I was barely making any friends, always wanting to keep my calendar open in case Max decided last minute that he wanted to hang out with me. I started to feel out of control in my emotions around him. Sometimes, after we'd have sex, I'd suddenly burst into tears, and he'd just stare at me, perplexed, as if having any emotions at all was an abstract concept. Or worse, simply embarrassing.

And then there was the sex issue. Max and I would have sex somewhat regularly—usually after taking a low dose of a psychedelic research chemical that he'd ordered on the dark web—but he generally just didn't care that much about sex. He was "above it," as he liked to say (he was also "above" food and friends and basically anything that one might derive uncomplicated and therefore unsophisticated pleasure from). But then randomly, one morning I found a pair of girls' underwear down the side of his bed. When I timidly brought it up, he insisted that they had been there "since before we met." To be fair, we had only been dating for about three months at this point, and his room looked like it hadn't been cleaned for three years. Also, we'd never had the "so we're not fucking anyone else" talk. But I mean, I didn't think it was necessary with him, especially given the conversation we'd had at my birthday dinner, when he spent forty-five minutes talking admiringly about this Russian cult of eunuchs known as the Skoptsy, who castrated themselves in order to be rid of sexual desire. "Once you are freed from sexual desire," Max told me, "or sexual desire is transmuted into work, suddenly the world becomes engorged with possibilities." Best birthday ever.

More often than not, when I initiated sex, Max would accuse me of not actually being horny, saying that I just constantly needed to be fucked in order to validate his feelings for me, and therefore validate myself. By this point in my life, I was highly experienced in being on the receiving end of this particular criticism. For years I had been told that my high sex drive was a sign of something darker in me, of desperation, a lack of confidence, a plea for attention. And while it didn't *feel* that way—especially with Max, given that I really cared about him—part of me couldn't help but start to believe it. But that's the way it goes, right? When a guy wants a lot of sex, it's because he's horny and thinks sex is fun, duh. But when a girl wants a lot of sex, it's like: "Bitch, what's your childhood trauma?"

And so, because I was weak-kneed and weak-willed, I attempted to subvert my own desires to match his—in life and also in sex. I told myself: *I've done the slutty thing; perhaps it's time to be the female eunuch.*

an atypical mentor

I was summoned into Malcolm's office one winter afternoon, by an email from his assistant. I already knew who he was. When I arrived he was sitting straight-faced behind a large oak desk, petting his Persian cat like a supervillain. "I've seen your films," Malcolm said to me, referring primarily to a video I'd made of myself masturbating on a fire escape in a fur coat, which I had put on the internet and called art. "They're good. You're interesting. I wanted to meet you."

Malcolm ran an erotic literary journal and hung out with porn stars, but still managed to be taken seriously because he was a man and dressed well. I assumed he wanted me to write for him, which was really exciting, considering that I'd been living in New York joblessly for three months at this point. Malcolm was British and nihilistic and twenty years older than me, and when he was taking care of himself, in certain lights, he could look James

Bond handsome. He and all his model ex-girlfriends had been heroin addicts in New York in the nineties, and hung around with Vincent Gallo and Harmony Korine. I was far too impressed by this.

"You should let me photograph you," he said, looking me up and down. "Nude."

I squirmed nervously in my chair. "Are you a photographer?" I asked.

"Not really."

"I'm not sure that's a good idea."

"Why not? Your tits are bad?"

"Uh…no, they're fine."

"Your ass then…is your ass bad?"

"No, it's fine."

"It's gotta be your pussy, then. Is it…" He made a *so-so* gesture.

Then came a long pause that was seemingly only awkward for me. His quiet confidence terrified me. "So, there's something I wanted to ask you about," Malcolm said, finally breaking the silence.

"My writing?" I asked.

He looked at me like I was an idiot. "I wanted to know, if we fucked, would you get weird afterward?"

"W-what do you mean by 'weird'?" I stuttered.

"Weird as in *emotional*," he said flatly, as if this were obvious.

"I wouldn't get weird," I answered too quickly. "Why, would you get weird?"

He thought about this for a moment, then shrugged.

"Maybe. But I get quite cranky when I don't get what I want."

We started fucking regularly. First once a week, then more often. (While Max and I still hadn't discussed monogamy by this point, this certainly deterred my ambition of self-castration.) Malcolm's apartment was directly above his office. I would visit in the late afternoons and he'd drag me from room to room by my hair, bend me over armchairs, tie me to the bed and hit me with a variety of expensive leather things. He loved to constantly remind me that everyone working in the office downstairs could hear my body being dragged along the floor, and ask me how it felt to take the L train back to "embarrassing Brooklyn" with cum in my hair. One of my favorite early texts from him read: *Be home at 8. Tired but would be good to beat u*. I cherished it like a love letter.

I liked that Malcolm was stereotypically sleazy, like the perverted boss from a shitty erotic novel or something. He liked to pull off my underwear and shove them down my throat while we fucked, or force me to blow him while he made important phones calls to…whoever. His casual pervertedness gave me license to emulate all the sleazy, over-the-top theatrical stuff I loved to watch in porn, like attempting to deep-throat while hanging upside down off a desk (although I would advise not eating kale salad immediately before trying this; it is not the food you want coming back up through your nose, believe me).

Fucking Malcolm was an entirely new experience for me. He was tall, with broad shoulders and a muscular frame, and I liked that he could pick me up and throw me around. Before him, every guy I'd dated was under 120 pounds, so the fact that he posed a legitimate physical threat to me made sex seem more…I don't know, significant? Essentially, he contradicted everything I thought I liked about men. And about myself.

Malcolm and Max were polar opposites when it came to sex. The couple of times Max had read my writing—which was only ever after I threw a tantrum about it—he had literally flinched with embarrassment. On multiple occasions he told me that writing about sex and dating wasn't "serious writing," and that the subject of sexuality was "girly"—girly, of course, being synonymous with "insignificant." But Malcolm loved my writing, and soon started commissioning me to write for his literary journal. He'd say stuff like "You're like Gore Vidal, if Gore Vidal was a slutty feminist blogger with a bad dye job." When I told Max about my longtime fantasy of sleeping with two men at once, he practically kicked me out of bed, saying that being fucked by two guys was degrading (meanwhile, I knew he wanted to have a threesome with me and another girl). But when I told Malcolm about my fantasy, his response was: "Baby, if you're good, I'll think about getting you a spit roast for Christmas."

Malcolm liked to jerk off while I told him stories about sneaking out of my parents' house in high school to fuck awkward skateboarders who weren't old enough to drive. The sluttier the story, the more into it he was. For most of my life, I'd dealt with people calling me a slut in a mean way. But with Malcolm, it wasn't *just* that he was turned on by my ho-ishness; it was clear that he respected it. It was a point of connection for us. Malcolm was the first person to make me feel like my sex life wasn't something to be ashamed of but rather part of what made me interesting—like my sluttiness was a sign of my curiosity about life.

Malcolm also loved making these grand, sweeping statements about my personality. Some of them were true, and some of them were certainly *not* true, but the ones that weren't sounded so good that I tried to make them so. For instance, he was constantly telling me that I was a sociopath, which I wasn't—I clearly had a ton of feelings, increasingly for him—but because he said it, I'd think, *Holy shit, I guess I am?!* "You're the purest sociopath I know," he'd say. "You don't beat yourself up about things that don't matter. You're like a shark—you don't think, you just keep moving." To this day, I think my general lack of regret is a result of him programming that trait into my brain.

Sometimes his feedback was less positive. For instance, he was always saying that I would be way hotter if I didn't wear such cheap shoes. He once threw a pair of my "hideous" Zara sandals out the window of a ten-story hotel and made me walk home barefoot. He started to dictate what I could and couldn't wear to our meetings. He once told me, "The next time I see you I don't want you to be wearing any of that hideous blue eye shadow. And I don't want you coming here in the underwear you've been wearing all day, either. From now on you should bring a fresh pair of underwear in your bag. Understood?"

I always said yes. Within a couple of months, I was doing almost anything he asked me to. It felt good to be so malleable. With Max it was different—I felt like I was drowning, like I was sinking under the weight of my emotions and he didn't even notice. But with Malcolm, my lack of power felt like a *decision*. I was in control of my submission, and it made me feel sane, somehow. Maybe I was like trauma victims who reenact their abuse through BDSM, and then it acts as a form of therapy—but with emotional abuse and manipulation? Who knows? Either way, I was learning that when you're in lust with someone, it's far more satisfying to be objectified than to be ignored.

Unsurprisingly, a lot of people thought of Malcolm as a perv (like, in a bad way), but they didn't know him like I did. In my eyes, he was the ideal male feminist. Not the self-congratulatory, condescending kind of male feminist who says shit like "*Sigh*, all of the inequality women face makes *me* so sad," and then treats you like a wounded bird in need of rescuing. They're the worst. Instead, Malcolm was the sort of guy who just didn't judge you, and who wanted you to be the most powerful version of yourself possible. And he understood that sex is a form of power.

Two months into our affair, Malcolm invited me on a trip to California, to help him work on an art book he was making. My job was to interview the artists, and his job was to, ya know, schmooze and smoke cigarettes and lounge around in his red cashmere slippers. It was our first time spending any real time together while fully dressed. We flew to San Francisco and stayed at the Fairmont, and all along the way he found every excuse he could to tell people that I was his wife. "My wife and I would like to upgrade our room. What's the largest bed you have? We might be having guests." I pretended to hate it.

My secondary job for the trip was to find us a girl for a threesome. I was only made aware of this upon arrival. "Technically you're working for me now, which makes me your boss, which means you have to do whatever I say," he said flatly, chain-smoking in the hotel robe. "It's my life's dream to get a blow job from two girls in Palm Springs while listening to Cher. Can you make that happen, baby, please?"

"But we're in San Francisco."

"Just make it work."

"But I don't know anyone here," I whined.

"*Ugh*..." He rolled his eyes. "What about all the insecure girls who read your blog? Won't one of them come over?"

I found this insulting, but also, like, potentially genius? I was still in that early relationship phase where I wanted to impress him. I wanted to come across like a skilled procurer. So I got out my phone and tweeted: "In SF, looking for guest star in a 3some tonight. Email pics." By dinnertime I had four replies. We passed my phone back and forth across the table, comparing nudes. I could tell he was pleasantly surprised. We settled on a tanned, voluptuous twenty-one-year-old who, like clockwork, showed up at our hotel at 9 p.m. and excitedly took part in our ménage, all to the soundtrack of "If I Could Turn Back Time." It really was perfect…minus the part where the girl got her period and I ended up with bloodstains on my bra and teeth, but whatever, menstruation happens.

Later that night, while basking in our post-threesome glow, Malcolm told me, "You really are good, baby. You're like a top whore. A prime fuck. You could make a lot of money doing this, if you wanted to." I had never felt so proud.

Unsurprisingly, I fell in love with Malcolm and wanted him to be my boyfriend. It seemed like the perfect way to segue out of my sort-of ongoing but ultimately destructive relationship with Max, who I was still technically dating despite the fact that sometimes I think he legitimately forgot I existed. Malcolm, unfortunately, did not agree. "*Come on*," I'd say to him. "We're perfect for each other."

"No we're not," he'd say. "And if you break up with your boyfriend, I'll stop fucking you."

Over the next couple of weeks, our relationship grew increasingly, shall we say, avant-garde. Back in New York, I got a call from Malcolm one evening telling me that his old friend was coming to town from London—a trip for his birthday weekend—and that Malcolm wanted to give me to him as a present. "You'll like him," Malcolm told me. "He makes hideous art that sells for a lot of money."

"What am I supposed to do with him?" I asked.

"Everything except anal. He's not that good a friend."

Said friend showed up at my apartment later that night. He was tall, blond, and unnervingly polite—like nineties

Hugh Grant, only somehow more apologetic. He drank water while I chugged wine, we made small talk, and then we had sex for like forty-five minutes. At one point, while we were fucking, I started to get off on the whole sex-as-currency thing, and I said something along the lines of, "You think I'm a whore, don't you?"—but like, in a sexy, dirty-talk way, so it sounded less embarrassing in context. Still, as soon as I said it, he suddenly froze, blushed intensely, and mumbled in his cute British accent, "Oh no, really, I don't think that. You seem like a nice, sweet girl, and I'm so enjoying spending time with you!"

Afterward I collapsed on my bed, my adrenaline still rushing. It amazed me how much I'd been into this scenario—I liked opening the door, not knowing who was on the other side, but knowing that whoever it was would get to do what he wanted with me. The idea that I was *a thing* that could be given to someone felt wrong and exciting at the same time. I wanted to be one of Malcolm's things—preferably stored in his closet and dragged out for periodic use. I couldn't tell if my sudden submissive urges were entirely new, or if they'd always been there, somewhere deep in my subconscious, and only now did I finally feel comfortable indulging them. Either way, I was going with it. The following afternoon I showed up at Malcolm's, excited to tell him about the previous evening.

"Can we do that again soon?" I asked him giddily. "With one of your other friends?"

He looked at me and smiled—one of those slow, satisfied smiles that your mom gives you when you wash the dishes without her having to ask. "You know what you are?" he said. "You're pagan. You live life virtually unencumbered by morals or values."

"I have values," I said defensively.

He shrugged. "That's what I love most about you: You have a genuine capacity for amorality."

It was the most romantic thing anyone's ever said to me.

is this degrading? (and do i give a fuck?)

You likely won't be surprised to hear that whenever I would regale my friends with tales of Malcolm and our sexy adventures, they tended to be vaguely horrified. The general consensus was that Malcolm was a pervert, and that the way he treated me was "degrading." Now, the pervert part I agreed with—but a pervert in a Tom Ford suit, which somehow feels less offensive?—however, the degrading part was something I never fully understood. That word, "degrading," is one that has come up in relation to my sex life many times over the years, before Malcolm was ever in the picture and since. But I never quite knew what it meant exactly. Can something be simultaneously degrading and fun? And if I enjoy things that are widely thought of as degrading, does that mean there's something wrong with me? Deep thoughts.

One of my first encounters with the term was in high school, when I was still a virgin. I was fourteen years old, riding the JV soccer bus back from an away game, when one of the older girls on the team decided to give us naive freshmen a sex talk. Amid other wildly off-base pieces of wisdom the elder shared with us that night (for instance, that giving a blow job with a flavored condom tastes like sucking on a lollipop) was the insistence that you should never let a guy fuck you doggy-style, because it's degrading. At the time, this made sense to me. If a guy cared about you, I thought, surely he would want to see your face while you were making love, right? Of course, age and experience taught me that you can be fucked from behind and still be a respectable human being (and that flavored condoms taste like battery acid). But experience has also taught me that sometimes the fact that a sexual act is a bit dirty or undignified is precisely *why* it's sexy. Like, isn't that sort of the whole point of doggy-style? That I want to be bent over and treated like an animal? As Jessa from *Girls* said after being told that doggy-style was degrading: "What if I want to feel like I have udders?"

A century ago, Sigmund Freud famously threw his hands up when confronted with female desire. Freud wrote, "The great question that has never been answered, and which I have not yet been able to answer, despite my thirty years of research into the feminine soul, is 'What does a woman want?'" Bro seemed to be confused about a lot of things female-related, but I'm with him on this one. It's roundly acknowledged by now that female sexual arousal is more complex than that of our male counterparts: Basically, (straight) guys are just happy to see boobs, whereas female sexuality is a messy tug-of-war between body and mind. We want romance, and yet we fall for guys who ignore us. We want security, but we also randomly have rape fantasies (admit it). We are feminists, and yet we're desperate for an older guy to spit on us and lock us in a closet. Have our vaginas gone rogue?

As women, we're told that being objectified is bad. Okay, fine. But there's a time and a place for everything. And if there's one thing I learned from Malcolm, it's that I personally can be very turned on by a skilled objectifier. It's no secret that women are often turned on by being wanted—not as in "I want to take care of you," but more as in "I want to bend you over my desk." Of course, when I'm dating someone, I want them to value me for my ideas and accomplishments and humor or whatever. But when I'm fucking someone, I want them to value my lack of a gag reflex. Within the context of a relationship or a hookup with someone who respects you, being treated like a sex toy can be really hot. Like, I don't always want to be a whole person. That's exhausting. Sometimes I just want to be my boobs.

And sexual objectification goes both ways. I remember, in middle school, my mother told me that there are three things I should always look for in a partner: He should be loyal, he should be handsome (but not too handsome), and he should be able to fix things around the house. She specifically noted that it's very important to find a man who can fix the sink when it's broken. I remember thinking, *Mom, you're basic*. But now I get it. It's not about the convenience of having an in-house handyman. It's about the simple fact that seeing a man hit something with a hammer is really hot. (Female gaze, anyone?) Sure, it's a gendered cliché, but there's truth in it—seeing a man be "manly" in a Don Draper, motor-oil-under-the-fingernails sort of way can be like porn. I guess everyone is basic at heart.

Malcolm was a master objectifier. On multiple occasions, he'd tell me to shut up and cover my face with a pillow, and then just basically fuck me like I was a decapitated RealDoll. But I was objectifying him, too. Sure, I cared about him deeply as a person—I loved our conversations, I loved the way his mind worked—but I also got off on the fact that he was this hot, older British guy in a tailor-made suit and a stupidly expensive watch, whose decadent apartment was aesthetically aligned with my Helmut Newton–esque sex fantasies. He was the perfectly cast pervert of my dreams.

Today, it seems like a no-brainer to me that being used for the sexual pleasure of another person can be really fucking hot. But it took me a while to get here. Unfortunately, the "Is this degrading?" question is difficult to escape as a woman. But why is this a particularly *female* anxiety? Is it because we have to work so hard to gain respect in real life that we prioritize a certain "respectable" code of behavior in the bedroom, even when it means sacrificing our own pleasure? And if that's the case, doesn't that suck? Just think of all the women who are currently not being spanked for the sake of their so-called respectability. A tragedy.

A few years ago, a girl in her midtwenties emailed my *Slutever* advice column, asking my opinion on facials (i.e., when a guy comes on your face). She said she knew that a lot of people find it demeaning, and wanted my thoughts on the matter. However, she seemed really confused when I told her that I had "no thoughts" on the issue. To me, asking, "What are your views on facials?" felt equivalent to asking "What are your views on bicycles?" They are both just things that exist in the world—you may like them; you may not like them; they might be particularly useful in certain situations, but ultimately neither of them warrants a political stance. There are certain matters in life that deserve careful consideration—like what lube to buy, for instance (can't risk fucking up your pH)—but some casual jizz on your face just doesn't feel like one of them to me. If you're having consensual sex with someone you like, and you're both turned on by the idea of him coming on your face, then what's the big deal? It's bad to analyze sex to the point where it loses its spontaneity and hotness. Perhaps we should all stop being so hyperaware of the sociopolitical context of our sex lives, and start focusing on other, more important things, like managing to have a fucking orgasm.

I understand that there are complex emotions involved in sex. But I also think that sometimes women's brains become so clouded by societally imposed values and "feminist" ideals—"thou shall not be treated like an object"; "thou shall always be offended by men's pervy remarks" (as if we are not equally adept at dishing them out)—that we spoil our own fun. It's definitely an "easier said than done" situation, but I generally try to remind myself not to take sex so seriously. (As my scary Russian bikini wax lady once told me: "Dick is not that serious.") I just think that, in the midst of doing something we want and enjoy, why stop and think, *Wait, should I be getting off on this less and feeling exploited more?* Talk about self-sabotage.

We determine what is or isn't degrading based on so-ciopatriarchal norms about how a woman should behave, which should make it obvious that the whole "Is this de-grading?" debate is just another way of policing women's bodies and behavior. But ironically, even though most women suffer under the degrading/not-degrading binary, it isn't just men who impose these constraints. There are a lot of women out there, and many who identify as femi-nists, who are quick to tell other women what they should and shouldn't do, and what is and isn't immoral or degrad-ing. (As bell hooks loves to say, "The patriarchy has no gender.")

About a year ago, I interviewed the legendary porn star and sex educator Nina Hartley. We were specifically dis-cussing a Netflix documentary called *Hot Girls Wanted* (2015), which follows a group of young women who are getting into the porn industry. The documentary, pro-duced by actress Rashida Jones, took a familiar, main-stream, puritanical stance on the situation—essentially, that female porn performers are victims, and that doing porn is degrading. One scene of the documentary that's particularly hard to watch involves a young woman shooting a scene for a site called Latina Abuse, which features "facial abuse" porn, where girls are face-fucked until they vomit. It did seem awful, and the film effectively made you feel bad for the performer involved. So I asked Hartley what she thought about it—specifically, is there a point at which we just can't deny that some sexual acts are degrading? And also, is it the business of a group of documentarians to make moral conclusions about the sex lives of a group of young women?

"Degradation is a subjective experience," Hartley told me. "Just because *you* don't find what's happening in a scene arousing doesn't mean the performers in the scene aren't having a great time…We watch these [facial abuse] scenes and we become outraged for her, we become concerned for her, and we become angry *at* her. But we don't know what is going on in her head. She may be going, 'It's so fucking weird and cool that I'm getting paid for this.'" Ultimately, according to Hartley, if a woman is consenting to something—be it doing extreme porn, or having a guy come on her face, or having her sort-of-boss pimp her out to his artist friends—that is *the woman's decision* to make. Hartley went on, "As a woman and as a feminist I have to give you the dignity of making your own choices, learning your own lessons, and not rushing in to save you from yourself. Because how patronizing is it of me…to rush in and say, 'Oh no sweetheart, you don't want that.' It's like, 'Fuck you!'

Men, on the other hand, almost never get told they are being degraded during sex. For instance, we never even think to discuss the male porn star who's doing the face-fucking. Like, is that degrading for him? Does *he* like doing that? Well, apparently no one cares, because men are somehow above sexual degradation and unable to have a sexual experience that isn't high five–worthy. But when a woman wants to experiment with engaging in extreme porn, as a performer or a viewer, somehow she always ends up the "victim" of the situation.

It should be self-evident, but the distinction between being a victim and not being a victim is consent. To quote one of my favorite porn performers and directors (and the creator of one of my all-time fave porn series, *Public Disgrace*), Princess Donna: "People don't understand that the main ingredient to everything is consent. I don't believe that there is any fantasy too extreme or too out there to enact between two consenting adults in a safe environment. I actually think that it helps people grow and become comfortable with who they are. And that little step to admit what you like in the bedroom will bleed over to the rest of your life and allow you to be more open with yourself and with others about what you need and who you are." To me, this is the ultimate slut scripture.

I watch a lot of porn, and have for years. Like many people my age and younger, I saw my first porn video while I was still a virgin. I remember once, after letting Malcolm tie me up in some insane Japanese shibari tie, he looked at me with wonderment and said, "Girls your age are amazing, because you're a product of porn." He was obsessed with the idea that the proliferation of porn had changed the way that people fuck, particularly people like me, whose initial concept of sex was largely formed by on-demand HD pornographic videos. Of course, this isn't necessarily a new or enlightened idea—if we copy the stuff we see on TV and in movies, why wouldn't we also mimic porn?

But it was funny to hear the argument from Malcolm's perspective, as someone who's been slutting around both pre- and post-PornHub. He said the biggest difference he's noticed is that today, women are turned on by things that don't necessarily stimulate them physically but instead excite them psychologically. "It's a mental thing," Malcolm told me. "They're excited by becoming something they've seen as powerful in a porn movie—they want to be 'that girl' who can deep-throat or whatever. When women my age were in their twenties, their image of a powerful woman was Princess Diana. For your generation, that woman is Sasha Grey." I'm not entirely sure if that's a good or a bad thing, but I don't think he's wrong.

Of course, pornography has long been one of the most controversial issues in feminism. But whenever someone tells me that porn degrades women, or that porn is sexist, I always just think, *That's because you clearly haven't seen enough of it.* When compared to other forms of media—like TV, movies, and fashion magazines—porn is far more diverse, featuring women of all body types, races, ages, and physical abilities. If there's one thing I've learned from porn, it's that literally no matter what you look like, even if you're obese and have one eye and are lying in a pile of hay in a barn, there's someone on earth who's going to want to have sex with you. And that's reassuring! I think that watching porn can be really good for women (and men) in terms of normalizing kinky or extreme fantasies, and also in terms of inspiring sexual confidence. Any world where you regularly see groups of men worshiping a giant ass full of cellulite is a world that I want to be part of.

Personally, porn helped me a lot with my body image when I was a teenager. I was a typical high school girl, perpetually obsessed with losing five pounds. I got boobs and hips before any of the other girls, and I felt insecure about it. I envied my friends whose thighs somehow still looked thin even when sitting in a chair. But then I saw the Pamela Anderson and Tommy Lee sex tape (this was literally the first porn film I ever saw, which I specifically remember took about four hours to download on our hellish dial-up internet) and suddenly everything changed. I quickly realized that I naturally gravitated toward watching porn where the women were more curvy, even so-called chubby, because their bodies had more bounce. I wanted to see flesh—girls with something to grab on to. Not that there's anything wrong with being skinny, but when you're fifteen and all your favorite magazines only feature models who look like baby aliens, porn is a welcome diversion from the norm.

Porn can certainly be problematic in the absence of sex education. Porn is sensational entertainment that's fun to jerk off to—it's not a how-to on making a woman come, and people need to be educated on that basic fact. But to make the blanket statement that porn is degrading to women denies the reality and complexity of female sexuality. Some women are exhibitionists, or like to play sexual power games, or get off on submission. Some women simply want to be paid to fuck (and to that I say: Respect, yo). Pornography is the ultimate representation of human sexuality—it reveals the deepest, most animal truth about our desires. Porn is democratizing. It teaches us what's on the menu. And it's just really fun to watch other people fucking, so, like, everyone chill out and let me live my life.

The seemingly inescapable "Is this degrading?" anxiety is so pervasive that not only does it influence our sexual behavior, but it even affects our fantasies. (Or at least, the lies we tell ourselves and others about what we fantasize about.) Have you ever noticed that when faced with the question "What turns you on?" almost all women have the same answer? It goes something like: "I'm turned on by someone who's smart, funny, well dressed, creative, successful," *blah blah blah*. Sounds suspect if you ask me. Sure, all those things are stimulating, but that's only half the story—frankly, the boring half. But I, too, often stick with the stock answer (at least when I'm in polite company), because saying some version of "I'm turned on by intelligence" sounds way less scary than the reality, which is that I'm mostly turned on by a weird genre of faux surveillance porn where teen girls are caught shoplifting and then blackmailed into giving security guards awkward blow jobs. Is that bad? I'm sorry, but I just don't believe that *anyone's* ever come thinking about how their boyfriend is a good listener.

Evolutionary biology tells us that what we find sexy is ultimately indicative of what's best for the survival of the species, meaning that being fit, having clear skin, and sending well-crafted emails—all qualities that evoke health and competence—make someone more fuckable. But can evolutionary biology explain my gang-bang fantasy? I guess the Darwinians would argue that sleeping with ten guys at once makes you ten times more likely to get pregnant, which is all part of my inherent desire to procreate. But I kind of don't buy that. All I know is that in order to come during sex, I usually have to close my eyes and focus extremely hard on the idea of being violated by a gang of meathead bros. Some might argue that it's a result of my growing up in Generation Porn. And yet, that fantasy certainly predates dial-up.

I remember the first time I read Nora Ephron's famous essay "Fantasies," when I was twenty-four. In it, Ephron discusses the rape fantasy that she's had since she was eleven. I was genuinely amazed that this woman—a feminist icon— had a rape fantasy, too. (You may remember that in Ephron's film *When Harry Met Sally*, Sally has the same fantasy; art imitates life.) Reading "Fantasies" was an intense moment of realization for me—like, *It's not just me? I'm not a lonely perv?!* It felt reassuring, but also slightly disappointing, if I'm honest. For years I had thought I was deviant in this special and unique way, only to find out that not only was I *not* a deviant—I was actually boring.

When "Fantasies" was first published in the early 1970s, it received some serious backlash. Liz Dance discusses the essay and its aftermath in her book *Nora Ephron: Everything Is Copy* (2015). Dance writes that Ephron's essay "provoked an outcry from some quarters, particularly by those in the Women's Movement who were outraged that Nora, a declared feminist, should write about rape fantasies. 'Fantasies' provoked criticism because Nora not only confessed to having a sexual fantasy, a rape fantasy in which she is 'dominated by faceless males who rip my clothes off,' but it was a fantasy that she thought of as 'terrific.'"

Essentially, these women defined Ephron's fantasy as not-so-feminist. Talk about perv shaming! The term "safe space" literally makes me want to barf, but in the classic sense, our fantasies—and our bedrooms, ideally—should be a safe space to act out our creepiest desires. And on that note, I don't think we need to file all our actions under "feminist" or "not feminist"—especially since consensual sex kind of exists in a political vacuum. It's pretty much the one place that we can just do things and move on, no angry think piece needed.

Clearly, I am a proud feminist. But I believe at its core, feminism is about freedom and a woman's right to make decisions for herself. And if that means masturbating to the idea of being mobbed by a group of personal trainers, or getting paid to deep-throat until you puke, so be it. One thing that's certainly *not* feminist is suppressing your desires because you think what you want is "just not something a respectable woman should do." As slut prophet Sasha Grey once said: "What one person sees as degrading and disgusting and bad for women might make some women feel empowered and beautiful and strong." Sometimes, in order to get to that place where we feel free to unleash our inner sex maniac, we have to kick feminism out of our fucking beds. Because at the end of the day, as long as we're not hurting anyone (who hasn't explicitly asked us to), then we should be free to have whatever type of sex we want.

in defense of sex maniacs

I do not always make the wisest decisions. I wish I could tell you that my perverted love triangle had a *Casablanca*-esque ending, where I was forced to choose between two men who loved me, and in the end chose Malcolm, because of the harmony of our sexual politics. Yeah, not even close. In reality, neither man seemed to care about dating me, but in a bizarre plot twist, I somehow ended up in a relationship with Max for the next two years. I guess opposites attract?

When I first met Malcolm, it was thrilling to be with someone so driven by sexual adventure. Put simply, he was a sex maniac, and that was a turn-on for me. In the years since meeting him, I have continued to be attracted to people of that particular breed—often called playboys, Casanovas, hedonists (or more recently "sex addicts"). For me, the turn-on is the idea that someone has no moral obstacle between them and their sexual desires, even if those desires sometimes get them in trouble. (Not to the point of harming someone, of course, but to a level of sheer stupidity is cool.) I think there's something about debauchery that's very liberating. There's just more on the menu when you're screwing a sex freak.

The trouble with sex maniacs is that they tend to make difficult or at least *challenging* partners. It wasn't easy being with Malcolm, even in a fuck-buddy-slash-romantic-friendship capacity. As time wore on, I naturally grew more possessive of him. Suddenly, his stories about the fivesomes he was having with a group of Norwegian fashion designers made me more jealous than wet. But I dealt with it—I mean, I knew what I'd signed up for. Until I hit my breaking point: the time he slept with one of my close friends, and was annoyed by the fact that I was annoyed. In our inevitable fight afterward, his defense was literally: "We weren't having sex. I was just teaching her how to give a blow job." Adding, "Really, it was more like a business meeting." How does he get away with this shit?

The demise of the affair was sort of inevitable. It's difficult to maintain that level of hedonism with someone, especially when you know that the sex isn't going to lead to an actual relationship, which Malcolm repeatedly made very clear to me. (Although he did once include the caveat: "Maybe, if you get famous, I'll consider impregnating you." Still crossing my fingers on that one.) He remained a friend—to this day we're very close, and continue to act as each other's default sex therapist—but there were no more sensual beatings, and pretty soon I was replaced by an American Apparel model.

Down one nonboyfriend, I started focusing more of my attention on Max. He could still be dismissive of my level of interest in sex, but we connected on other levels. We could talk for hours, we made each other laugh, and I loved how after we fucked I would be covered in tiny circular bruises, simply from making contact with his bony frame. I've never met a man so pointy; it was truly a dream. And Max did start making more of an effort to be supportive of my writing. Like the time when he bought me the textbook *Sexual Deviance: Theory, Assessment, and Treatment*. It would have been better if he hadn't followed up the gift with, "Maybe you can learn something…*about yourself*." But still, I think his heart was in the right place. And in the moments when he did inevitably launch into critiques of my psyche, I felt newly capable of dismissing his criticisms. My relationship with Malcolm had armed me with a newfound slutty confidence. Like: "I'm not traumatized, I'm just a sexual cosmonaut, hello?!"

Strangely, when I was still seeing Malcolm, he would often give me advice about Max. Once, while I was rambling through my usual list of complaints about our relationship—about how Max would ignore me, and how he would refer to me insultingly as "blogger brain," Malcolm suddenly interrupted and said something that kind of changed the game for me. "Look, darling," he shot back. "Allow me to explain this to you. Your boyfriend has a superiority complex, which means that he obviously doesn't feel very powerful in the world. He's just a bully. But you obviously care about him, so I wouldn't let it get to you."

"Well, if I care about him, then why am I sleeping with you?"

He rolled his eyes at the apparent stupidity of this question. "Because you love him so much that it makes you feel powerless, and fucking someone else makes you feel in control. Obviously."

The reality of that statement was dizzying. "But he's mean to me," I whined, because I couldn't think of anything better to say.

"Well, next time he's mean to you, pick up a knife and stab him."

Max and I broke up when I was twenty-seven. I never used a knife on him, though I thought about it many times. The reality was, Max wasn't enough of a sex maniac, I was potentially too much of one. Also, it was just difficult to date someone who refused to leave his apartment. After the breakup, I did what I always do when a relationship ends: I went on what I like to call a "rebound rampage," which is where you basically just have sex with anything nearby and remotely sentient. It's pretty much a no-fail breakup cure. This time, however, my rampage was a little more, shall I say, *rampagey* than usual.

A mere week into my new single life marked the now historic Saturday when I fucked five people in less than twenty-four hours (and not at a sex party, which would have been cheating). That morning, I woke up with a nightmare headache, still wearing my PVC party dress, in a hazily familiar penthouse at the St. Regis New York. I was immediately handed a Bloody Mary by my new prostitute best friend, Madeline, who had thrown a party there the previous evening. Madeline then promptly coerced me into a threesome with another leftover party guest— a real estate guy in his forties who had apparently paid for the room. (For a moment I questioned whether the threesome was actually payment for the room, but he was really handsome, so I just went with it.) So that was two before breakfast. Then came a lunchtime relapse with Malcolm, followed by a quickie in the bathroom of an uppity Park Slope house party with my friend's husband's brother, and then I finally ended my record-breaking day by crawling into bed with a Spanish lesbian who I'd been clinging to for dear life since my first moment of singledom (who intuitively forced me to shower before reluctantly agreeing to finger me).

Following my rampage, I felt weirdly proud of myself— like, "Wow, that was an unusually productive Saturday! Have I just *fully* actualized my slut potential?" But another part of me couldn't get that line from Max out of my head. You know the one: "The hole you're trying to fill is not in your pussy, your ass, or your mouth. You need to figure out what's missing in your life and tend to it, otherwise you're just going to end up fucking yourself into oblivion." (That line is so good, by the way— totally worth enduring a two-plus-year abusive relationship for.) Something about this particular rampage felt like it was crossing a line, even for me. Because as I've often wondered throughout the course of my sexual experience: How much is too much? At what point do you go from being a hedonistic, thrill-seeking neoslut to having a legitimate problem? What constitutes too much sex (an amount we're supposed to feel bad about), compared with the appropriate amount of sex, compared with not enough sex (which we're also supposed to feel bad about)?

It's not just sluts, or even just women, who question this. Of course, we all know about the sexual double standard. However, as much leeway as we give men when it comes to promiscuity, there *is* actually a limit to how much sex we let men get away with before we start vilifying them, too. Having *a lot* of sex with *a lot* of different partners is typically criticized across genders, though the criticisms differ slightly. It tends to go like this: If you're a man who sleeps with many different women, you're generally thought of as being kind of an asshole, an unethical player type, or, worst case, a predator. Whereas if you're a woman who has a lot of sexual partners, then you must have "issues." Basically, as Max so eloquently put it: There's a gaping hole in your life, and you're trying to fill it through your pussy.

It's not only old people or religious extremists who think this way. Even young folks today are pretty divided over whether casual sex with a lot of people is okay. While the nebulously defined Millennial generation has liberalized on a lot of issues that our parents were weird about—

for instance, having premarital sex and being gay—having casual sex with many different partners is something a lot of us are still not *really* down with. A Cornell University study surveying 24,000 undergraduates throughout twenty-two different colleges all over the United States found that 60 percent of students said they would "lose respect for a man or a woman who hooks up with a lot of people." Despite the vast social progress our society has made in recent years, we're still having growing pains when it comes to sex outside the confines of long-term romantic relationships. But aside from the social stigma, is there any actual evidence to say that having a lot of sex with many different people is, in fact, bad for you?

To answer this, I went to Dr. Zhana Vrangalova, a doctor of psychology, professor of human sexuality at NYU, and pioneering sex researcher on the topic of casual sex and its link to mental health. Dr. Zhana also happens to be one of my closest friends, which meant that it was easy to sit her down over bowls of ramen in order to pick her enlightened brain for answers to all my slutty questions.

Zhana noted that while there is a long-held puritanical assumption that having sex with many people is harmful for both sexes, there's actually little data to back this up. "Casual sex has many potential benefits," Zhana told me. "For instance: sexual pleasure; an increased sense of self-confidence, desirability, and freedom; and satisfaction of our biological need for adventure. Study after study finds that people have more positive reactions after hookups than negative ones. Other studies show that casual sex has little or no impact on longer-term psychological well-being, meaning things like self-esteem, life satisfaction, depression, and anxiety."

In her TEDx talk "Is Casual Sex Bad for You?" Zhana makes the argument that whether casual sex can be good for your psychological well-being depends on *who you are* and *how you do it*. So, obviously, the next question becomes: How do I know I'm of the slut genotype, and how can I tell if I'm slutting around in the right way? Zhana broke it down for me, starting with *who you are*.

So, we know that sexual orientation exists on a spectrum. This is often evaluated using the Kinsey scale, which measures a person's sexual orientation on a scale of 0 (exclusively heterosexual) to 6 (exclusively homosexual). What you may *not* know is that there's also a sluttiness spectrum—surprise! The proper name for this is not, unfortunately, "the slut scale" but rather *sociosexual orientation*, which measures how oriented a person is toward casual sex, ranging from highly restricted to highly unrestricted. If you have an *unrestricted* sociosexuality, that means you're someone who desires a lot of casual sex, you like fucking randoms, you crave novelty, maybe you sometimes casually fuck five people in a day (hi!), et cetera. And if you're someone with a *restricted* sociosexuality, that means you're not interested in casual sex, you don't think about it, and you might even think sluts are immoral monsters.

The 2014 Cornell study "Who Benefits from Casual Sex? The Moderating Role of Sociosexuality," (*Social Psy-*

chological and Personality Science, 2014) examined the influence of sociosexuality on the psychological well-being of single undergraduates following casual sex encounters. The study, conducted by Dr. Zhana, found that unrestricted students typically reported higher well-being and lower levels of depression and anxiety during the weeks when they got laid compared to the weeks when they didn't. However, for the restricted students it was the opposite: In the weeks they hooked up, their well-being suffered. So the message is pretty clear: Not everyone is wired to be a ho.

God, I wish someone had told me this sooner! Life would have been so much easier if I could have blamed my sluttiness on science, rather than some apparent lack of self-worth. It also would have potentially made dating a lot more straightforward. Like, when you think about it, it's bizarre that, starting when we're really young, we're told to seek out a partner who we're compatible with—someone who's interested in the same things that we are, who's equally ambitious, and who shares a similar vision of the future. And yet nowhere along the line did someone think to say: "Oh, and also, you should probably choose someone who has a similar level of sluttiness to you." That tiny piece of advice could likely prevent a plethora of sexually mismatched marriages. And personally, I'd like to think this knowledge could have steered me away from dating people who seemed fundamentally less interested in—or even dismissive of—sexual exploration. Or at least it could have helped me give context to my sexual interests and behavior, making me less vulnerable to the critique of partners—and people in general—who didn't approach sex in the same way that I do. But maybe that's delusional. When I want to fuck someone, I'm rarely thinking rationally. Although, who is?

But back to Dr. Zhana and the science of sluttiness. Now that we've addressed the *who you are* part, let's try *how you do it*. Zhana stressed that motivation is a huge factor in the outcome of our hookups. Based on self-determination theory, a well-established theory of human motivation and personality, we know there are two types of motivations for the choices we make in our lives: autonomous and nonautonomous. Extensive research shows that when we do things for the "right" (autonomous) reasons, our well-being flourishes, but when we do those *exact same* things for the "wrong" (nonautonomous) reasons, our well-being suffers. And that's pretty intuitive—like, *choosing* to have sex because you're horny or sexually curious, or because the dude looks like Louis Garrel, usually leaves you feeling glamorous and in control, whereas hooking up with someone because you were depressed or feeling ugly can leave you with a shame hangover. The bottom line is that, when identifying unhealthy sexual behavior, what's critical is not the *amount* of sex we're having, but rather how and why. One can have a lot of sex in a healthy way, and a very small amount of sex in an unhealthy way. And that's something I've certainly learned firsthand.

I'll preface this story by saying I'm not a person who

regrets very much (potentially thanks to Malcolm's brain-washing, as previously mentioned). I understand that regret is useful in that, in theory, it prevents us from making the same mistakes over and over. But it's also often an unnecessary form of self-punishment. Ideally, we would just learn from our mistakes and move on, lest we risk ending up in "woe is me" victim purgatory. However, there *have* been a couple of specific instances when I've regretted my sexual behavior, times that felt particularly destructive, and as Zhana predicted, my regrets came from my motivations to fuck, rather than the body count.

The time that most sticks out in my mind was when I cheated on my ex-girlfriend. Alice and I had been dating for more than a year, and were in a monogamous stretch of our relationship. We were going through a rough patch, and I was feeling jealous and anxious about her continued friendship with a girl who she'd been sleeping with back when we first met and were trying an open relationship. Turns out my anxiety was warranted, because I woke up Christmas morning to a text from Alice confessing that she'd cheated on me (being a Jew, she lacked respect for Jesus's b-day). I pretty much wanted to die, and spent the following weeks drinking myself into oblivion, crying in bodegas, and just generally feeling like an emotional train wreck. Eventually she and I worked it out, and we decided not to break up over it. I told her that I could forgive and move on. Those were apparently lies, because a month later I was still a hot mess, boiling with rage and resentment. So one night I went out, drank a million tequilas, and went home with this ex-Mormon filmmaker lesbian, *specifically* because I wanted to get back at my girlfriend. I was in full-on drunken cunt mode and wanted revenge. But afterward I thought, *Wait, who am I?* Not because the sex was bad—the girl was cool and hot, and we continue to be friends today—but I felt disgusted with myself because I was out of control. My emotions had gotten the better of me, and I was having mindless, detached sex out of spite with the intent of hurting someone I cared about. That is certainly not classy slut behavior.

Once, Malcolm told me that the greatest sexual quality is composure. It sounds slightly off base at first. Adjectives like "wild" and "deranged" feel more obviously sexy, as compared to "God, he's so composed!" Plus, this assertion seemed especially counterintuitive coming from a sex maniac. But eventually I've come to agree with him. Composure in the bedroom isn't about putting restrictions on yourself, or only fucking missionary or whatever—it's about knowing how you want to fuck, making autonomous decisions, and getting the most out of sex. There's this stigma that sluts are "out of control," but that's not always the case. You can be a hedonist and still have composure. You can be a sex maniac and also be a decent human being who communicates your desires in a way that doesn't offend anyone. You can be a slut with poise. You can even, so I've heard, be a slut with morals! You just have to get the dance right.

Of course, any conversation about "right" and "wrong" reasons to have sex can get messy, because what's right for one person isn't going to be right for everyone. I, like many people, grew up in an environment where I was told that I should only have sex for love (and only after I was married, as if that task weren't already impossible). Today, most of society has moved away from that extreme, but we are still living in the hangover of that morality. We're often told that sex should be driven by romance and a deep emotional connection—that you should only fuck someone if you care about them (at least a little bit). And I agree that that's a great reason to fuck. But who says that romance has to be what motivates us to have sex? Why can't we have sex simply because we're bored, or stressed, or because we're broke and sex doesn't cost any money (at least, usually)? Or because we want something to talk about at a dinner party? Or because I just broke up with my boyfriend and banging my personal trainer sounds like way more fun than crying while ordering Seamless?

That said, I don't think Max's critique that I try to feed my ego through my pussy is totally off base. I'll admit that at certain difficult points in my life—periods when I was dealing with a lot of work stress, or after a breakup or whatever—I would turn to casual sex as a distraction, or as a quick and easy form of validation. And maybe those aren't the absolute *best* reasons to be sleeping around, but it's not the worst way to deal with a low period, either. I have friends who turn to alcohol or drugs during particularly rough or stressful times—not to the point of addiction, but to a point of excess, as an escape.

So why is it "wrong" to use sex as a coping mechanism?

If sex is something that makes me feel good, then of course I'm going to seek it out at times when I'm feeling shitty. And maybe it doesn't fix things, but it's still useful. They say the best way to get over someone is to get under someone else. Well, certainly for me, after breakups, casual sex has been a very welcome distraction—a pillowy segue into singledom, and probably ultimately more healthy (for me) than pounding martinis and Xanax.

Sex has connected me to people in myriad ways. Sure, at points it has fueled and intensified my romantic love for someone. But sex has also been so much more than that for me. It has made my life more dynamic. It has been a shortcut to intimacy. It has been a source of rebellion and provocation, as well as a continual form of entertainment—for myself, but also for other people, given that I've literally made a career out of ranting about it. But also, sex has made me seem more interesting *to myself*. It has colored my personal narrative. Over the years, I have come to see my sex life as a marker of my curiosity and my freedom (granted, with a little help from a sadistic older man). It has become an integral part of the personal story that I tell myself about who I am. It's like Joan Didion's famous adage: "We tell ourselves stories in order to live." Or more like, we tell ourselves stories in order to fuck. Or even better, we fuck in order to tell ourselves stories.

sadomasochist in training

chapter 3

book bitch

I *met my slave online*, where I meet all my friends.

It was the winter of 2010 and I'd been living in New York for just a couple of weeks. I'd yet to make any money or friends—save for Max, who was more of an infatuation than a friend—so I spent the majority of my time alone in my apartment, staring at the internet. Around that time, there was this random dude from England who kept sending me Facebook messages asking if he could buy me stuff. He looked normal. Creepily normal, in fact—the sort of person who you don't notice even when you're looking at them. He was in his early thirties with a dad-bod, brown hair, nondescript clothing, and that vaguely inbred-looking face that all British people have. He'd send me messages like "Hello there Your Highness, is there anything you need that I can buy for you?" I figured he was trolling me. However, after numerous emails of this type, I figured I might as well see if this dude was for real, so I sent him an Amazon wish list of books that I thought would look impressive on my shelf, in case my pseudoboyfriend ever came over. Sure enough, within a couple of hours he'd cleaned out my wish list. I was like...*word*.

Pretty soon, I was receiving books from this dude in the mail almost every day. In return, I'd send him photos of myself reading them (and occasionally licking them, when he asked nicely). It was pretty simple. But not so surprisingly, things turned bizarre pretty quickly. I clocked that something unusual was going on the day he sent me a video of himself on all fours, crying, begging to buy me more books. Then came a series of selfies of him with *BOOK BITCH* carved into various parts of his body, smiling and holding up a bloody knife. And then there were the excessive TL;DR emails he'd send, telling me that I owned him. He was coming on a bit strong.

At the time, I *sort of* knew about BDSM, but only vaguely. Remember, this was pre–*Fifty Shades*, back before every basic bitch on the planet kept a leather paddle in her handbag. I mean, I wasn't *totally* clueless. I had pretended to read the Marquis de Sade in high school. Plus, I had that weird experience with the self-righteous house-cleaning slave from the squat. Thanks to that, I had a general understanding that there are dudes in the world who get off on doing mundane tasks for apathetic women. Also, given that I wasn't raised in a black hole, I was familiar with the aesthetics of bondage, which have been present in culture in various forms over centuries. I had long been a fan of the photographer Helmut Newton, whose decadent and erotic images marry fashion and fetish. I'd seen iconic photos of gay leather daddies from the fifties, and Robert Mapplethorpe's images of hot gay guys dressed up in latex, piercing each other's buff bodies. And let's be real, I grew up Catholic—the stations of the cross is basically BDSM 101. Essentially, I had a Tumblr-level understanding of sadomasochism.

As pathetic as Book Bitch was, I really have him to thank for introducing me to the world of BDSM (which is a compound acronym that incorporates bondage and discipline, domination and submission, and sado-masochism; and sorry if that goes without saying). It didn't take long for the relationship between Book Bitch and me to evolve beyond Amazon wish lists and self-harm videos. Soon he started begging to pay my rent. (Well, begging is probably an overstatement; I didn't take much convincing.) Turns out, Book Bitch was a cash pig. Also known as a human ATM, or a pay pig, or a money slave. Translation: Book Bitch was into financial domination, which is an element of dominance and submission (D/s for short) in which a (usually male) submissive gets off on giving money and gifts to a financially dominant woman (also known as money mistress, findomme, or money domme). In other words, Book Bitch was the holy grail of slaves. Like, an average email from him would read: "Take my money, please Karley! I want you to have it, PLEASE. I'll send it right now, please don't say no!" Subtlety was never his thing.

Book Bitch began PayPal-ing me rent money in weekly installments, in exchange for degrading emails and Skype humiliation. Who knew that treating someone like shit could actually make them like you *more*? (Actually, I'm pretty sure that everyone knows that. Cue Max.) The humiliation was primarily centered around him having a tiny, inadequate dick. (His dick was actually normal size, but he asked me to pretend that it was tiny, and once confessed that he was actively looking into penis reduction surgery.) So I'd be like, "Your penis is basically invisible." And he'd be like, "Here's a hundred dollars." It was all very sophisticated.

At first I was just amused and vaguely grossed out by him. But unexpectedly, in the weeks that followed, we developed what I suppose could be called a friendship. Or at least, we would confide in each other quite a bit, which I guess is what friends do? For instance, I'd talk to him about how the guy I was dating didn't want to have sex with me, and he'd tell me about how he couldn't have sex with a woman without crying. Or he'd regale me with stories, like the one about the time he was meant to go see MGMT with a prostitute he met on a fetish forum, but then she didn't show up, so he stood in a corner by himself, creepily smiling at strangers and wishing he had friends. Or the one about the fifteen-year-old girl whose phone bill he was paying, who (ironically) wouldn't answer his phone calls. His stories were unanimously depressing, but on the plus side they made my life seem less tragic in comparison.

Our Skype sessions tended to follow a similar routine: For the first ten minutes he would jerk off while I told him he was pathetic and would never get a girlfriend. Then, after he came, I'd ask him questions about his cash pig exploits. A typical Friday night for Book Bitch generally went down like this: He'd start chatting with a woman on a fetish forum, he'd meet up with her at an ATM, and then she'd force him to get down on his knees and take out £300 for her. And that was it. That was his passion. Another one of his hobbies was to show up at a restaurant at the end of a woman's date and pay the check for her and her boyfriend, and then he'd go home and jerk off. He said the amount of money he gave to women per month was directly proportional to how often he got horny. When he was getting laid regularly (so basically never) he barely gave away any money. But the more he went out drinking, the more horny he would get, and the more often he'd wake up in the morning and realize there was £500 missing from his account. He said that some of the people he sent money to online were definitely men posing as women, but that usually he was too horny to care. (I mean, gender is over anyway.) (Just kidding.)

Sadly, a couple of months into our friendship, I received what was essentially a breakup email from Book Bitch, saying that he'd been laid off from his job and couldn't afford to send me money for a while. (What is it with slaves dumping me?!) He also hinted at the fact that I was never very good at insulting him, and that I was "too nice" (translation: a bad dominatrix). I was hurt...sort of. But our relationship had sparked my interest in the world of BDSM, and as a parting gift, Book Bitch gave me the contact information of a prominent New York dominatrix, saying that if I really wanted to learn the ropes and become a good sadist, I should spend some quality time with her. And this is how I came to meet the woman who would change my life, for better *and* for worse: Mistress Daisy.

peeing my way to the top

The first thing I learned from Googling Mistress Daisy was that she's "New York's reigning queen of forced-bi." Forced-bi, I also discovered, is when you make straight guys suck cock as a form of degradation, and since not all dommes do this, it's sort of a big deal. She seemed impressive. So I decided to call up the Mistress to ask if I could tag along with her for a few days, hoping that the experience would help me decide if the dominatrix life was truly what God or Satan or whoever had always intended for me. To my surprise, she said yeah, she would love to have me. She said quite a few of her clients were into having "civilians" observe their sessions—I guess it adds to the humiliation factor—so this arrangement could work out for her, too.

My first visit to Daisy's home was on a Tuesday afternoon to watch what her email described as a "1-hour in-person w/ male submissive." She answered the door wearing a sheer red thong and nothing else. Wavy chestnut hair, porcelain skin, *huge* tits for someone so petite. "Cool, you're not ugly," she said, and motioned for me to come in.

The first thing you notice after entering Daisy's apartment is the chandelier hanging at the center of the spacious living room, made entirely of glass butt plugs. As I walked in, a cool breeze came through the open window, causing the butt plugs to clink together, making a pleasant chiming sound. The walls of the room were lined with metal meat hooks, like the interior of a slaughterhouse. On one wall sat a large antique cabinet with glass doors, full of a combination of sex toys and torture tools. There was one shelf for dildos (there must have been a good twenty or thirty in there, all shapes, sizes, and colors, including one terrifyingly large black dildo that looked capable of damage I was reluctant to even imagine), one shelf for gags, one for masks (including a pink latex balaclava), one for whips, and so on. On the wall opposite, where most people would have probably put, like, a couch, sat an authentic stainless steel autopsy table. "A dominatrix friend of mine bought that at some sort of morgue-going-out-of-business sale," Daisy explained casually, "but she ended up giving it to me because it was creeping out her roommates." She paused, thoughtful. "It really comes in handy—ya know, autopsy fantasies, zombie role play, and my personal favorite: necrophilia fetish." Later on in our friendship, Daisy would blame the interior decoration of her apartment for the fact that she'd been single for more than five years.

"Just to warn you," Daisy said between swishes of Listerine, "the guy that's coming over sort of looks like a troll. Like, he's old and short and has this weird hunchback thing. I think it might be scoliosis? Whatever, he's harmless." She pulled a black latex dress with military epaulettes, and matching latex knee-high boots from her closet. The dress was so impossibly tight that she had to cover her body in lube in order to get it on. Daisy was pretty in a 1930s movie-star kind of way, with a face that seemed to belong to another time. She reminded me of Audrey from *Twin Peaks*, only sluttier. "Oh shit, I forgot I have to piss on him," she said, and ran to the kitchen to chug three glasses of water.

When the doorbell rang, Mistress Daisy instructed me to hide in the bathroom and not to come out until she said so. She said the slave didn't know I was coming, and that she wanted him to be surprised. So I sat waiting in the bathroom with my ear pressed against the door, feeling either excited or just nauseated—it was hard to tell. Soon I heard what sounded like a belt being undone and shoes coming off. I heard Daisy's muffled voice saying, "I did a three-hour dungeon session last night, and these boots are *filthy*." A few minutes later she called my name and I emerged from the bathroom feeling sort of like a stripper popping out of a birthday cake. What I found was the slave naked on all fours, aggressively lapping up the myriad day-old bodily fluids from Daisy's boots. He crawled over to me, panting and drooling, and kissed my bare feet. "You can kick him if you want to," she said. I told her I was fine for the moment. "Suit yourself." She shrugged. "I was just trying to be a good host."

Daisy reached into her cabinet of pain and pulled out a tool consisting of two parallel metal bars clamped together at their ends. She then grabbed the slave's balls and pulled them back toward his ass, clamping the base of his scrotum into the center of the bars, which sat horizontally behind his thighs. "Now try and stand," she said teasingly, after which he made a feeble attempt to extend his legs, only to collapse to the floor in pain. This happened a few more times, each collapse followed promptly by a "Thank you, Mistress." Eventually she pulled what was left of him up off the floor and rode him around like a horse for a while, giving him some vague verbal encouragement but mainly just looking absently at her nails. What surprised me most about Daisy in that first meeting was her demeanor. She wasn't super angry or serious; she never raised her voice or yelled. Rather, she was really giggly and relaxed and self-aware, which seemed at odds with the image of the evil, man-hating sadist that I'd always imagined a dominatrix to be. She sort of flipped back and forth between being really "in it" and being obviously bored. At one point she was literally whipping the guy's balls with one hand and texting with the other.

Somewhere around the half-hour mark, Daisy led the slave to the bathroom and ordered him to lie faceup on the shower floor. I sat on the toilet and watched as she crouched over his wrinkled body and began pissing into his open mouth. Her bladder control was impressive, to say the least. She had this incredible ability to pee until the exact moment that his mouth was full to the brim with urine, stop and wait while he swallowed, and then begin her flow again with total ease. It was really amazing to watch. Only once did a tiny trickle of pee escape his mouth and drip down his cheek, at which point she shouted furiously, "DO NOT WASTE ANY OF MY PRECIOUS URINE!" The slave apologized profusely.

Somewhere in the midst of the urine therapy I found myself thinking, *Wait, is this, like, weird or gross or something?* I quickly decided that yes, it was gross—but like, gross in an endearing way? I tried not to overanalyze, and went back to taking dorky notes on my very journalistic notepad. When she was done peeing, Daisy shoved her foot far down the guy's throat and thanked him for being a "good little toilet." The look on his face could only be described as pride.

In the bedroom, Daisy and I shared a box of Godiva chocolates on her bed, resting our legs on the back of the slave, who had positioned himself to be our footstool. However, because of his hunchback situation, his body formed a stool that was more rounded than flat. "Oh my god, drop your hunchback down!" Daisy shouted, her mouth full of chocolate. "We literally have to crane our legs to rest them on you...Ugh!" And then she just laughed and popped another chocolate into her mouth, like, no big deal.

For the session's finale, Daisy ordered the slave to jerk off onto a paper plate, then proceeded to spoon-feed him his own come, swooshing the jizz-filled spoon around like an airplane—like you see mothers do with their toddlers—before shoving it into his mouth. I breathed through my nose, silently telling myself not to puke. As it turns out, watching a man consume bodily fluids for an hour is incredibly nauseating—at least, until you get used to it. This, I would soon learn, is the reason that BDSM dungeons require new dommes to undergo what's called a "desensitization period" before they can be officially hired for a staff dominatrix position. It's pretty much basic training, only far from the type that my dad had always planned for me. It essentially involves sitting on the sidelines during sessions led by other dommes until you're able to watch a man gargle urine without either passing out or vomiting (a valuable life skill, no matter your profession). Vomiting on the job isn't chill because it breaks the illusion that you're "into" whatever kinky shit you're being paid to do to/for your sub. Unless, of course, the sub pays you to barf on him—known as a "Roman session"—which is a different story.

After the session was over, the slave excused himself to shower and get dressed, and soon emerged with a bright smile, passing for a totally noncontroversial member of society. But before he left he got down on his knees and thanked Daisy. This thank-you was different, less role play, more honest. You could tell that the past hour had truly been of value to him. That somehow, being reduced to a human toilet was exactly the medicine that this man needed.

Maybe reading this today, in a world where you can literally buy a whip at Victoria's Secret, everything I just explained seems like old news to you. But at the time, the idea that someone could make a living by peeing into the mouths of random investment bankers was pretty shocking to me. And it was all so casual, like these dudes just leave on their lunch breaks to go chug some pee and then head back to Goldman Sachs or whatever. That's funny, right? It makes me feel better about the world somehow. And while it wasn't like I had some crazy revelation after that first session—no lightbulbs went off inside my bladder—I was definitely intrigued. And so began my desensitization period.

Later that week, I showed up at Daisy's to find her midsession with a middle-aged Hasidic Jew who, she'd previously informed me, was into public humiliation and chastity. He was naked except for a pair of zebra-print panties and some studded leather handcuffs. Daisy was applying red lipstick to his pursed lips, saying over and over, "What a pretty little slut you are!" Underneath his thong, the guy's dick was locked in a plastic chastity belt, the pressure of which had turned his balls the color of raw meat. This guy was a lot more playful and smiley than the previous slave. Like, he could easily have been your favorite science teacher in high school, or your goofy landlord (for a second I was like, *Wait, is that my landlord?*). I can't explain it, but I sort of wanted to give him a hug.

The three of us left Daisy's apartment and walked to a nearby sex shop. Inside, Daisy ordered the slave to take off his coat, then scribbled the word "SLUT" across his chest in red lipstick. They browsed the store together, picking out a pair of fishnet thigh-highs and a rainbow penis lollipop. At the checkout counter Daisy gave him a knowing stare, and he immediately burst into song, singing a little jingle that had obviously been composed in anticipation of this moment.

I've got all holes available
Tell all your friends I'm salable
I want to be used, abused, bent over your dinner table
A faggy slut with all holes available

The slave sang this through a couple of times, looking sort of embarrassed but also like he was about to come. The cashier—an apathetic black guy—was completely unfazed, like he'd seen this a million times. "*All riiight*, man," he said, nodding in slow motion. "*Whatever* you say."

Back at the apartment, the slave put on his new stockings and showed them off by twirling around the room like a ballerina. Daisy unlocked the guy's chastity belt and I watched as he jerked off and came onto the penis lollipop, which Daisy then forced him to eat. And I didn't even gag this time! Turns out watching dudes guzzle their own cum is a lot like Adderall—you build up a tolerance really fast (but if you do it too much you'll likely end up in a psych ward).

In the week that followed, I watched Daisy put a grown man into diapers and pretend to breast-feed him. I watched her stick needles into a man's scrotum and feed dog treats to a guy who was like seventy-five. Before Daisy, I had known about the existence of dominatrixes, who I understood to be women who inflicted some sort of physical and/or emotional pain onto (mostly) men, and that while these experiences were sexual in nature, they (usually) didn't involve actual sex. But the reality of seeing my first BDSM sessions was just so much more, like...*funny* than I ever imagined. It felt playful and inclusive. One of my naive assumptions that was immediately debunked was that the role of a dominatrix was simply to abuse people in whatever way she saw fit in the moment. Sort of like improv theater, except with more pee. In reality, sessions are catered to a client's specific desires, and in order to be a successful pro-domme you have to straddle the line between being an in-control bitch and accommodating what your client wants. It's a tricky balance. The way Daisy handled it—which, I've come to find, is a common method among dommes—was to ask the client before a session to describe his ultimate fantasies and his hard limits. This tactic gives the domme an idea of the sub's mental landscape, so that in the session she can address the things she knows they want, and then throw in some tangential surprises without crossing any of their hard boundaries. You always have to do *enough* of what the client wants, because if you just tell them to fuck off and then do whatever you feel like, they're probably never going to hire you again, and you're going to be broke. But most dommes are more likely to accept clients who present their desires in a subservient way, like "I enjoy being trampled" or "I would be honored if you trampled me," rather than "Ho, trample me."

Subs can be picky, demanding little bitches. Whenever I saw a sub get bossy with Daisy I'd always think of this one scene in the movie *Choke*: the protagonist (played by dreamy Sam Rockwell) meets a woman in a Sex Addicts Anonymous meeting who has a rape fantasy—as well as OCD. She wants to role play a rape scenario, but she wants to micromanage every step of the rape, and during the role play she's constantly pointing out all the ways that he's raping her wrong. In the kink world, this type of naggy sub behavior is often called "topping from the bottom." Daisy pointed out that, while it's generally good to challenge systems of authority, like in a "fuck the patriarchy" kind of way, in her dungeon, a slave who didn't know his role would fall victim to the ultimate punishment: no piss for a week.

What was intended solely as an apprenticeship quickly turned into a friendship between Daisy and me. I think she appreciated that I was nonjudgmental and curious, but mainly she liked that I was quite obviously in awe of her. At the end of the week, after I watched four sessions as an overenthusiastic civilian, Daisy offered me a job as her assistant. She'd pay me fifty dollars an hour to stand next to her during sessions wearing a leather bra, hand her butt plugs whenever she needed them, and—when the mood felt right—to chip in on the abuse, like a good sadist-in-training. Who knew you could get such a great job without a college degree? And at the peak of the financial crisis, no less!

For my first day on the job, the plan was to beat up and

then pee on a police officer. (It sounds too cliché to be real, but that's pretty much the case with everything in the BDSM world.) I turned up to Daisy's wearing the most fetish-looking outfit I owned: a black pleather skirt from high school that I'd since gotten too fat for and a black tank top with lots of zippers on it that was supposed to look bondage but was realistically more Claire's.

"So we're going to start with what's called a beat-down," Daisy said excitedly. "Do you throw a good punch?"

"No."

"Well, it's not hard. Just make a fist and swing. No hits to the face, though—focus on the stomach and ass. We can't leave marks; he's got a wife."

I asked Daisy what would happen if I got stage fright during the golden shower—like if I couldn't *go* when it was time to go. "Don't worry about it," she said with a shrug. "I'll pee first, and the sound of my pee will make you pee." It seemed like she knew what she was talking about.

As it turns out, there's actually a science to pissing on someone. If you start chugging water too early, then you end up struggling in pain for the entire session, feeling like you're going to explode (or at least give yourself a UTI). However, if you start drinking too late, then you might only have a couple of measly drops when it's time to go, which could lead to a bad Yelp review, so to speak. Knowing when and precisely how much to drink before a golden shower is an art, perfected over years of practice and dedication—think yoga, but with your bladder.

By the time the cop showed up it was clear that I had made the rookie mistake of drinking too early, and was literally gripping a dildo with my inner thighs for dear life, which Daisy assured me is a tried and true method of "keeping it in." The guy was around forty with broad shoulders, a red face, and a neck that seemed to be receding into his body. As soon as he walked through the door, Daisy began ripping his clothes off, punching him at the same time. I held his arms behind his back while Daisy cut off his underwear with a pair of scissors. My adrenaline was spiking so hard that I didn't even realize that tiny drops of urine were trailing down my legs. Between blows the cop was making overly dramatic cries like, "Oh God, someone please help!" and "These women are abusing me!" I felt like I was an actress in a really bad porno.

After about ten minutes of continuous beating, Daisy ordered the cop into the bathroom. Surprisingly, I felt more relieved than nervous. We all squeezed into the shower—the dude on his back, Daisy straddling his face, and me hovering over his stomach. I started peeing before I even had time to fully pull my underpants to the side. Daisy looked up at me, eyes glowing, which I knew meant she was impressed. Daisy started peeing, too, and as the slave gargled our piss we gave each other a high five. I felt oddly proud.

As the cop got dressed he made some jokey comment about how he was going to have to hide his torn underwear from his wife. He said never in a million years would she imagine that he would do something like this, and at the moment she thought he was shoveling snow. He'd considered telling his wife about his kinky side many times over the years, but he could never bring himself to do it. Daisy just smiled and nodded and let him talk. And as he continued to blab away to her in this obviously cathartic release, it suddenly occurred to me just how important Daisy was to all of these people. She wasn't just some hot chick who they paid to mutilate their balls; she was their escape. She saw them at their most vulnerable, she knew things about them that their wives and coworkers and friends would never know, *could* never know. And they really needed her. She was their therapist. Their confidante. The one person who knew what went on in the darkest corners of their minds. It's like she was God or something, if God were a babe in latex.

mind games

Mistress Daisy had pretty high standards. I didn't. This meant that whenever Daisy had a request for a session from a client who seemed super annoying, or like a potential serial killer, she would just pass him on to me, knowing that I was desperate and would do pretty much anything for money. We made a good team.

Daisy's sloppy seconds were my only clients. I was okay with that because I was never really interested in launching my own career as a pro-domme ("pro" meaning professional, as in you get paid for it, rather than just doing it because you're naturally a monster). Becoming a successful dominatrix in your own right is no different from becoming successful in any other industry—it can take years to make contacts, gain a reputation, and grow your business. You have to devote time and money to making a good website, doing fetish photo shoots that represent your personal brand, and integrating yourself into the fetish scene through kink parties and online forums. You have to advertise your services on fetish websites, which is another big cost. If you can't work out of your apartment then you have to rent out commercial dungeon spaces to session, and you also have to invest in the wardrobe and props, which aren't cheap—a quality flogger will cost you between $150 and $300, and the only latex dress I ever bought was $350. (Not only was that dress my most expensive article of clothing, it was also pretty much equivalent to my yearly salary back when I was squatting, just six months earlier.) Basically, you don't just become a successful dominatrix overnight, even if you have connections in the industry. I didn't see myself being in the BDSM scene for long enough to devote the required effort to launching a solo career, and so in the meantime I was totally content with being a bottom-feeder.

After assisting Daisy for about a month, I felt confident enough to do a few sessions without her. Because I was thrifty (read: poor) I bought most of my torture tools from Home Depot rather than at a chic sex shop, and I hit up Petco for my dog collar and dog bowl. (I was slightly embarrassed about this at the time, but have since learned that it's somewhat normal protocol. I once heard a domme in San Francisco sincerely refer to Home Depot as "Home Dungeon.") However, since Daisy tended to think it wasn't worth her time to see someone for just a half-hour piss session, most of my solo sessions ended up simply involving golden showers. Because I lived in a decrepit Bushwick apartment with two craigslist hoarders, I couldn't work from my apartment, so I would rent out a room in a dungeon on Thirty-Third Street, above a studio that held pottery classes. The room cost me $30 for a half hour, and I'd charge clients $150, so I'd be making $120 to essentially just empty my bladder. This felt fair to me, since I emptied my bladder all day long for free anyway. There was a solid year of my life where the vast majority of my income came from peeing into the mouths of middle-aged men, which I admittedly found quite glamorous.

But the most memorable client that Daisy passed on to me had no interest in my bodily fluids. This guy's name was Steve. He'd been pestering Daisy for sessions for a while, but she could never really work out what he wanted from her. "He doesn't even seem like a sub," she told me. "He seems more interested in playing these weird psychological games. He's, ya know…twisted. Scary. Potentially dangerous." I called him up.

Steve was fifty, bald, smiley, and very thin. He walked with a cane to help counteract his severe limp, the cause of which he described only as "a disease that will probably kill me." Steve and I met for lunch in Midtown, and he immediately started talking about how his wife was cheating on him. Recently, he told me, he had hacked into her email account, printed out all the e–love letters she'd exchanged with her side ho, and then scattered them around their house. His wife's response to this passive-aggressive outing was to flush Steve's erectile dysfunction medication down the toilet. "Flushing your Viagra," Steve told me, "is the modern-day chastity belt." I sat there, scarfing steak and Prosecco, nodding at appropriate intervals.

Steve told me that he had a "friend"—a twenty-year-old aspiring model with fiery red hair and freckles—who he wired money to occasionally, as financial support "until she gets famous." At some point, the Aspiring Model had led Steve to believe that she would fuck him—someday. However, after six months of his buying her gifts and giving her cash, she'd yet to put out (she once let him massage her back in a hotel room, but that's as far as it got). Now, Steve said, he was fed up and wanted to give the Aspiring Model a reality check. "She needs to be shaken up a little," he said assertively. This was where I came in.

Steve's plan was as follows: He would take the Aspiring Model out for a nice dinner. Afterward, he'd lead her back to a hotel room, offering her a massage. Once in the room, I'd show up and start banging on the door, pretending to be his wife and screaming bloody murder. He'd open the door and I'd threaten to kill both of them, and then (one assumes) she would run out crying. After a couple of days of radio silence, he would tell the Aspiring Model that he could no longer support her, now that his wife had discovered their secret pseudoaffair. Steve hoped that after he threatened to take the Aspiring Model off the payroll, she would finally bang him in an effort to change his mind. I asked Steve why he didn't just threaten to cut her off now, and save the effort of the whole fake-wife hotel-meltdown moment. He just shrugged, spooning caviar into his mouth. "But where's the fun in that?"

Steve said that if I could pull this performance off, he would give me $500. I was *slightly* offended that he felt I could believably play the role of his wife, given that I was half his age and considerably less creepy, but I agreed nonetheless. While I did feel vaguely bad about being an accessory to the manipulation of the Aspiring Model, it wasn't bad *enough* to keep me from making an entire month's rent in a single night. As they say: Shelter before hos.

So, the following week I showed up at the Plaza and downed an extortionately priced vodka soda at the bar while waiting for Steve's text telling me it was showtime. While I waited, I tried to channel the anger I had felt the time I'd found a pair of women's underwear in Max's bed, only a month earlier (a trick I'd learned back in drama class during that embarrassing period when I wanted to be an actor). Eventually, I got the "action" text and headed to the elevator.

Maybe it was my makeshift method acting, or maybe it was just the vodka, but as soon as I started banging on the hotel door, I really got lost in the moment—I *became* that cheated-on wife, pounding my fists on the door and screaming, "Steve, I know you're in there! Open up! I know she's in there with you!" I got so carried away that

I unexpectedly went off script, yelling about how I'd read his texts and was going to chop his dick off Lorena Bobbitt style and then feed it back to him—a line I'd stolen from Daisy, but still, I thought it was a good ad lib. Eventually Steve opened the door and I stormed in, wielding a mascara wand and threatening to kill him, as planned. I came in just in time to see the Aspiring Model running into the bathroom. I followed, still screaming, to find the freckled waif cowering in the shower. She literally looked twelve, which was awkward. Steve eventually crutched in and started threatening to call the police, in what was some of the most appalling acting I've ever seen. I felt like I was trapped in one of those slow-motion sepia reenactments you see on late-night crime shows, except somehow even less believable.

The awkwardness escalated quickly. After the initial burst of rage, the energy in the room suddenly crashed, and then I was just left standing there like... *Uh... okay, where is this going?* I looked to Steve for help, at which point he broke character and started clapping and shouting, "Bravo! Bravo!" with a big stupid smile on his face. I just stared at him, confused and sweating, as the Aspiring Model crawled out of the shower, looking seasick.

"Wait, what?" I finally said.

"You were great!" he said, laughing manically, endlessly amused by the bizarre scene that he'd masterminded. Basically, Steve had told the Aspiring Model ahead of time that I was going to come and pretend to be his psychotic wife, so really they were setting *me* up. I didn't understand the point of this at all—and still don't—but Steve was loving it. He was pounding his cane and laughing so hard that he was gasping for air, as if he were having some kind of senile orgasm-slash-seizure. The Aspiring Model just shrugged at me apologetically. I was too confused to be embarrassed, and for the next half hour the three of us awkwardly drank wine together on the bed, while the girl showed us images from her budget modeling portfolio on her phone. While this was unlike any other BDSM role-play scene I'd ever experienced—and while I was clearly not the domme in the scenario—I still left feeling pretty pleased. I mean, there are worse ways to make $500.

A couple of weeks later, Steve got back in touch, saying that he wanted to play another game. A part of me wondered if I could trust him, but another, less sensible part was curious about what other scenarios would emerge from his warped imagination. Also, on some level, I knew whatever we got up to would make a good story. I mean, I'm a writer: I'll do pretty much anything for an anecdote.

This time the game seemed pretty simple. Steve was going to put up an ad on craigslist, offering a girl $200 to have lunch with him at Le Cirque. My job was to sit at the bar and wait for him and Craigslist Woman to walk in. After about five minutes, I'd walk over and pretend to recognize him from work, and then I'd awkwardly invite myself to join their table for lunch. This was really when the game began: My challenge was to try to get the girl to agree to have a threesome with us by the end of the meal. (We were never actually going to have the threesome, Steve insisted—I just had to get her to *agree* to it.) If I could manage this, I would get $500. If I couldn't convince her on the threesome, I'd only get $200. Conveniently (and somewhat bizarrely), Steve was not the first middle-aged man who'd given me the task of organizing an impromptu threesome with a complete stranger. Since I'd succeeded with Malcolm, I was confident that I could make it work again. This was literally one of the only professions on earth for which I actually had job experience.

The plan started off smoothly. I lurked at the bar in the back of the restaurant, drinking a Bloody Mary, and watched as Steve and the woman—roughly thirty, heavy makeup, beige stiletto knee-high boots—came in and sat down. A few minutes later I clumsily inserted myself into their conversation, and quickly pulled up a chair. The girl seemed annoyed that I'd crashed their lunch, but also relieved that I was picking up the brunt of the conversational work. She kept looking at Steve like he was a bug that needed to be squashed, which made me feel oddly protective of him. I tried my best to steer the conversation toward sex. "So, are you two dating?" I asked. I think I saw the woman gag. Steve, on the other hand, was oblivious. "Well, I *could* be dating if I wanted to," he said too loudly. "My soon-to-be-ex-wife filed for divorce a year ago. And yet we still share a bed, because she wants me to massage her shoulders! She's making a mockery of the institution of divorce!"

It wasn't going so well. "So how do you guys know each other?" I asked.

"Well, I suppose this *is* a date," the woman said reluctantly, realizing she should probably work for her food. I then launched into a series of boring and never-ending anecdotes about how my boyfriend had just dumped me, how I was lonely, and how it was so nice to hang out with the two of them because they were such good listeners, and a bunch of other lies. And then, in what was probably a complete non sequitur, I was suggesting a threesome for the table. The woman looked me up and down, assessing my motives. "I mean…sure, I guess so," she said, dead-eyed. For some reason my response was simply "Thank you."

Steve, blushing intensely, then launched into an awkward rant about the logistics of transportation to and from the threesome. "I'm happy to pay for your Ubers to my hotel," he told us, unable to make eye contact. "But one of you might have to get your own Uber and then I'll reimburse you. Ya know, I think Uber needs to launch 'Uber Threesome,' to enable you to order more than one car at once. How am I supposed to organize a threesome through Uber if I can only order one Uber at a time? It's a flaw in the system."

After the woman left—presumably unknowing that she would later be ghosted—Steve was giddy. "She wanted you *so badly*," he said. "She was *so* attracted to you."

"No," I replied. "She is obviously just a prostitute and thinks she's going to get paid. Didn't you also pay her to have lunch?" Steve agreed this was a likely possibility, but still, there was pride in his eyes.

Part of me liked that I never knew if I was going to be in on Steve's joke or if I'd be the butt of it. Like one time, I went to meet him for lunch, but it turned out he'd scheduled lunch with both me and a twenty-year-old stripper, and then he just never showed up. When I texted him, saying that I didn't want to have lunch with this random stripper, he replied, "But she's a pageant queen! A former Teen Miss Northern Suburbs of Illinois! Impressive!" (I looked it up, and that pageant is somehow real.) I was annoyed, but then the waitress brought over a bottle of Champagne and a note from Steve saying he'd pick up the check. I have to give it to him—he does have a bizarre intuitive quality, because the lunch actually turned out to be kind of fun, and I ended up interviewing the girl about stripping for my website. But what could Steve have possibly gotten out of that? I liked the idea that he was just sitting home alone, jerking off to the thought of me and the budget pageant queen eating Cobb salads, comparing slutty notes.

My best guess was that Steve was being half-willingly cuckolded by his wife, and in the absence of sex, he got his erotic kicks by freaking out girls from the internet, in order to exercise revenge on the female gender, which had tormented him for most of his life…or something? He was definitely deranged, but I really took a liking to him. After the games began, he and I would meet for lunches a couple of times a month, and he'd read aloud the explicit emails that his wife would send to her lover, which always centered around the prowess of this man's supposedly "perfect pink cock." He would read really loudly, making sure the people seated at nearby tables could hear him. (Remember, this is an extremely sweet-looking disabled man that we're talking about.) "Can you believe the stuff my soon-to-be-ex-wife is sending her boyfriend?!" he'd shout at me across the table. "She met him on JDate! I found her profile, and she lies about her age! She also uses a photo of the two of us, with me cropped out! I paid for her boobs, and I never even get to see them—the irony!" He loved to play the victim.

The fact that I knew Steve's wife was a serial cheater was what absolved my feelings of would-be guilt for the time he paid me $300 to masturbate in their bed while she was out to dinner. "Make a mess" was his only instruction. He didn't watch, but he was delighted at the thought of his wife coming home and getting into bed that night, oblivious to what had gone down. I reminded myself what Daisy had told me once: If you ever start feeling guilty about a client's wife or partner, just remind yourself that if it wasn't you, it would be someone else. As I sat there with my vibrator, I tried to imagine other women in this position. What type of woman ends up with this as her job description? I wondered. And more important: How did this end up being *my* job, and even weirder, why was I randomly so good at it?

I realized quite quickly after entering the world of kink that whenever I encountered a new fetish or turn-on or perversion, I was instantly intrigued—I wanted to know *everything* about cash pigs or pee fetishes or whatever it was. But then as soon as something seemed old hat—as soon as I became desensitized to it, so to speak—I no longer cared. It was the same story with Steve. Steve's puppeteering got old pretty fast. I think he suspected that I was losing interest, because he tried to up the ante. Soon after the marital-bed-discharge incident, I got an email from him that read as follows:

> I've lined up some entertainment for us. She's a Russian giant—over 6 feet tall! She wanted to meet me at the cemetery last night—at midnight! Apparently, if she appears naked on her mother's grave in front of two strangers, under a full moon, and the body is above 50 degrees (F), her mother will get out of purgatory and into heaven. So time is of the essence. I checked this assertion in the Russian Orthodox Bible and the Koran and it is true. So, I brought a meat thermometer (for roasts). While this is a bit macabre and bizarre even for me, time is of the essence. We only have a few more days to make this happen. Your thoughts?

All relationships have an expiration date. For me and Steve, it was the moment when he asked me to stick a meat thermometer into the corpse of a Russian giant's mother, while her daughter straddled her grave, naked. Again, I reminded myself: *If not you, it will be someone else.* This time, I was happy to admit that I was not the woman for the job.

the hostage

It was the fall of 2011, and Daisy and I had been working together for about a year. I was feeling pretty confident in my knowledge of kink by this point—in fact, I was starting to get a little tired of BDSM altogether. I mean, how many times can you watch a Hasidic Jew lick his cum out of a dog bowl before you start to get bored? (Turns out it's actually three times.) I needed to spice things up.

This is why, when Daisy called to ask if I was interested in being one of her accomplices in a kidnapping she was orchestrating, I was immediately all in. This, Daisy assured me, would be by far the most intense D/s scene I'd done to date: the realization of an abduction fantasy. "This is a great opportunity for you," Daisy told me. "I mean, how many times in a woman's life does *she* get to play the rapist?" I laughed awkwardly, assuming that was intended as some sort of slutty feminist bonding moment.

For most people, the idea of being abducted, held hostage, and tortured is obviously terrifying. But in the BDSM world, one person's nightmare is another person's mental masturbation reel. While working with Daisy, I'd heard her talk about kidnappings she'd organized in the past. She often boasted about the time she managed to kidnap a guy on a busy street in central London in broad daylight. Two of Daisy's hired henchmen threw a bag onto the victim's head as he walked out of his law firm on his lunch break and tossed him into the back of a van, without any witnesses attempting to stop them or call the police, simply because Daisy was standing nearby with a makeshift sign that read STUDENT FILMING IN PROGRESS. It's pretty genius, really. When I asked Daisy if she had been nervous while the kidnapping was going down, she responded condescendingly, "I've literally buried someone alive." For my own sanity, I assumed that it was a consensual burial—and that she dug them back up again.

On a phone call, Daisy informed me that for our kidnapping the hostage would be an Indian-American banker in his early thirties, who was shy and with a slight build ("easy to throw around"). The cost of his kidnapping, which he had paid up front, was $3,000. He'd given Daisy information about where he worked, where he lived, and the route he generally took on his commute. He knew that he was going to be kidnapped at some point in the coming weeks, but didn't know when exactly it would happen. This is what Daisy was famously so good at: the element of surprise. She told me that I would be working with her and a third dominatrix, assisting in the kidnapping and ensuing torture. I was so excited that I forgot to ask for any specific details about how exactly we were going to execute this whole abduction situation. In hindsight, this was a *major* oversight on my part.

Given that humans are freaks, it may not surprise you that abduction fantasies are actually pretty common. Studies show that between 30 and 60 percent of women, and a somewhat smaller percentage of men, report having had these types of fantasies—abduction, captivity, forced sex—at least once. (To reiterate, your rape fantasy doesn't make you interesting, sorry.) For some, the desire to be abducted is about giving up control—about being able to say, "I didn't want to suck all those dicks, someone *made me* do it, so it's not my fault!" In our culture that represses sexuality, being *forced* to do something sexual absolves you of any potential guilt. And as perverse as this may sound, being the object of desire plays a big role in rape/abduction fantasies. If someone wants you *so badly* that they're willing to break the law and all social norms in order to have you as their sex toy, then they must *really* want you. There's also the fact that abduction scenes often incorporate elements of kink—submission, masochism, humiliation, forced sex, pain, fear play—so as a sub, you're really getting your money's worth.

While it's common to have fantasies of abduction and rape, it's not common to make the effort to have these fantasies realized. Abduction scenes are not your everyday request as a domme, and these role plays are not for BDSM beginners. Far beyond the typical requests for spanking, bondage, and humiliation, abduction fantasies require intensive planning and rule making, and can play out over months of blackmail and harassment before the final abduction. Often up to four or five people are required to execute the actual kidnapping and subsequent torture. Basically, if you're making your abduction fantasy a reality, it means that you *really* want it to happen. To an outsider, it might seem silly—or straight-up idiotic—to commit so much time and money just to be thrown into the trunk of a car and then hit with sticks by some bossy bitch and her slutty interns. But then again, think about how much money, effort, and time we put into other aspects of our lives—like birthday parties, backpacking around Europe, juice cleanses, a meticulously vegan diet…for *your dog*. It's weird how we think it's valid to spend so much time and money on those embarrassing things, but to devote equal resources to satisfy one's sexual needs seems crazy. Who knows: Maybe if I spent less money on my personal trainer and more money on being locked in a closet by a stranger, I would be a happier, healthier person. Fortunately, I'm not brave enough to test that theory.

But back to Daisy. I showed up at 5 p.m. at an apartment building in the Financial District, which was owned by Daisy's dominatrix friend, who was acting as the third kidnapper. Daisy was wearing black leather pants with a black leather jacket and a black leather baseball cap and black leather gloves and looked literally insane. The other domme and I had been instructed by Daisy to dress like "civilians," and were wearing jeans. Then there was a fourth woman, an old Asian lady who looked extremely out of place. She was introduced to me as the getaway driver.

"Okay, so which one of you wants to carry the gun?" were the first words out of Daisy's mouth. This, unsurprisingly, was when I started to panic. Daisy then pulled out an actual, real-life handgun from her bag and demonstrated that it wasn't loaded by shooting a series of blanks at the floor. I, being the self-defined least insane person in the group, then launched into a tirade about all the reasons why carrying a gun on the streets of Manhattan a mere four blocks from the World Trade Center memorial was literally the stupidest thing a person could do. But Daisy just kept rolling her eyes and telling me not to be a baby. I looked to the other domme for help, but she just excitedly grabbed the gun and shoved it into the crotch of her pants. So that was that decision made.

"No one is going to see the gun," Daisy assured me. "And if anyone gives you any trouble, just say you're shooting a student film."

"But we don't have a camera," I pointed out—an observation that everyone else seemed to think was irrelevant.

The plan was to intercept the Hostage on his way home from work. The other domme and I would approach him with a subway map, pretending to be tourists in need of directions. As soon as we had his attention, my accomplice would pull out the gun "discreetly," concealing it from passersby with her coat, and press it into the Hostage's side. We'd then lead him down a nearby alley, where Daisy would be waiting in a doorway, ready to pull a bag over his head, put him in handcuffs, and shove him into the trunk of a car, which would be driven away by the Asian grandmother. She would drive him around the block a few times to disorient him, until we eventually brought him back to the apartment in which we were currently standing. My accomplice and I would be waiting outside, and when the getaway car pulled up we'd get the Hostage out of the trunk and lead him upstairs, where Daisy would be ready to commence the torture.

"Just remember," Daisy said, "it's *not* illegal to pull someone out of the trunk of a car in Manhattan."

I told her that wasn't at all reassuring, but no one was even listening to me anymore.

Somehow, the abduction started off smoothly. My accomplice and I approached the Hostage and asked for directions to the 6 train. He was sort of cute, with slumped shoulders and a baby face full of zits that made him seem too young to be wearing a suit. As soon as he tried to point us in the right direction, the crazy domme pulled the gun out of her crotch and shoved it into his side. I then linked my arm with the Hostage's, girlfriend-boyfriend style, and led him into the alley. As we walked, my body pressed against his, I could feel his heart pounding fast. Mine was pounding, too, but the fact that the gun-wielding moment had gone smoothly meant that my terror had subsided…at least slightly.

Twenty minutes later, the grandma pulled up to the apartment. As soon as we stopped, my accomplice and I quickly began to yank the man out of the trunk. What happened next is exactly what you'd expect to happen when two people pull a man with a pillowcase over his head and his hands tied behind his back out of the trunk of a car four blocks from the World Trade Center: We were immediately ambushed by plainclothes police.

I was tackled to the ground by one of the officers, while the other held back my accomplice, leaving the victim standing confused, screaming into his pillowcase. I then, as instructed, began shouting, "We're making a student film!" over and over again. Somehow, despite our lack of cameras and the fact that my accomplice was like forty-five, this instantly calmed the officers down a bit. (That trick is amazing?) The cops, who were taking turns telling us to be quiet and to explain ourselves, then dragged us to the sidewalk, unbagged the Hostage, and began a mini interrogation, to the horror and amusement of the Wall Street bros passing by us. The officers asked the Hostage if the student film story was true, and thankfully he played along with the lie. When they asked us why we didn't have a camera, he even ingeniously improvised that this was a rehearsal. The cops *sort of* seemed to buy it, but they still took down our names and information and reported the incident, so this is probably on my record somewhere. I, of course, was silently panicking, worried that the officers might discover the gun hidden in my accomplice's vagina, but thankfully we weren't searched. Instead, they just told us that we were really stupid for pulling someone out of a trunk in the Financial District at rush hour—student film or not—which is an assessment I fully agreed with.

Eventually the cops let us go, after which my accomplice and I awkwardly brought the Hostage upstairs to her apartment. I then started yelling at Daisy about us nearly being shot and/or arrested, to which her response was simply "That's crazy" followed by "Does anyone have to pee?" I sort of did have to go, actually, so we tied up the Hostage and put him in the bathtub, and then all of us peed on him at the same time. Then I watched Daisy torture him for a while—including forcing him to send dick pics to his ex-girlfriend—which was admittedly pretty funny. However, while watching her hang half of the Hostage's naked body out of a fifteenth-floor window, I had a moment of realization: *This is fucking crazy.* I left before I got the chance to feministly rape anybody. On the train ride home, I decided it was officially time to look for a new job.

okay, but why, though?

After I first met Daisy, the following year of my life became pretty consumed by BDSM—learning the ropes (literally), making some money from it, and meeting and talking to people in the community to try to answer one essential question: "Why do you do this, and what do you get out of it?" Or more to the point: "What the fuck is going on inside your head?"

I should probably admit that most of the practices that fall under the BDSM umbrella don't really turn me on. While I'm definitely into sexual power dynamics—I'm a natural sub, and love being told what to do—it's hard to separate BDSM from its aesthetics, and I'm just really not into all the props and the leather and the latex, or those ridiculous red velvet thrones that seem to be fucking everywhere. Kink parties felt too performative to me, and I just got sort of awkward whenever I was in a dungeon, like an actress who'd been thrown onstage without memorizing her lines.

I know a lot of people disagree with me on this, but

I can't wrap my head around role play. It just hasn't ever worked for me. Of course, I acknowledge that certain triggers—whether they be verbal or aesthetic or otherwise—can help to stimulate the sexual imagination, and add to a fantasy or sexual experience. Like, I lose it for a guy in a suit. It's an aesthetic that's representative of authority, which helps to heighten the power dynamic for me. I've also just recently realized that I'm one of those creeps who can get off on calling a guy "Daddy." But all the fetish paraphernalia, the costumes, and the theatrics that are involved in most BDSM play just kill my boner, because I can't get myself to buy into it.

Although, I *do* love a good spanking (so long as the spanker has enough natural authority to be convincing). I've spent a considerable amount of time wondering why I like being spanked so much, and the answer I always come back to—which is so obvious that it's cheesy—is that growing up, being spanked was a punishment I got for being "bad," and I have always gotten off on the idea that I'm doing something I'm not supposed to do. (It's not a very sophisticated motivation, I know.) But that's pretty much the extent of my sadomasochistic appetite. (Oh wait, I actually do sometimes like being tied up. But that's not a BDSM thing. That's just a being-lazy thing.)

Despite not wanting to sleep in a cage at the foot of someone's bed, after becoming a sort-of-domme, I became increasingly interested in why *other* people like this stuff. And looking back, this newfound curiosity was a major turning point in my writing career. Up until then, my writing on *Slutever* was primarily oversharey rants about my own sex life and relationships. But the kink world made me realize how interested I was in the sexual behavior of others, and the psychology surrounding fringe or extreme sex practices. And quite plainly, my involvement in BDSM led me to have some of the most entertaining moments in my life. Like the time I went to a fetish wedding at the famous New York dungeon Pandora's Box, and watched the bride, a molecular biologist, walk down the aisle in a white latex wedding dress and be tied to a Saint Andrew's cross (one of those giant X-shaped crosses you see in most dungeons, named after the diagonal cross that Saint Andrew is said to have been martyred on). Then, rather than having a ring put on her finger, she had her dress pulled over her head and her clit pierced with a diamond in front of roughly fifty people. I mean, not many people can say they've done that. In a sense, BDSM made me into a pervy voyeur. Sex became more than just sex—it was a spectacle, a tool for provocation, and a way of connecting with people, even if I wasn't fucking them.

Over the years, I've met dommes who approach BDSM similarly to the way I do: Kink doesn't necessarily get them wet, but it stimulates them in a different way— it's more an arousal of the ego than the clit, so to speak. Daisy was quick to admit that she didn't always find domming sexually arousing, but that emasculating men made her feel high, powerful, capable, and in control. It was an adrenaline rush, and it increased her confidence. About domination she once told me, "It's better than a fucking orgasm. It's female supremacy at its finest." She also was known to say, "I blow my load during every session—intellectually."

Of course, there are plenty of dominatrixes out there who are naturally dominant, and their dominance crosses over into their personal sex lives. But in my experience, the vast majority of dommes will tell you—in a sort of "Okay, but don't tell anyone I said this" way—that with their off-the-clock partners, they prefer to be the one being spanked than to be the person doing the spanking. Or they prefer to just chill the fuck out and have lazy boring sex where no one goes home with a black eye.

Before Daisy, I had been naive about the world of kink. Like most people, my idea of BDSM basically went like: "Oh yeah, those freaks in basements who pay lesbians to pierce their dicks because they hate their dads"…or something. Not *entirely* false, but also pretty far from accurate.

Sure, in a lot of ways, the reality of BDSM is true to its clichés: Yes, it does involve a lot of girls with dyed black hair and short bangs hitting people with paddles. Yes, there *are* a lot of high-powered Wall Street guys who like to indulge in cock-and-ball torture after a long day of making money. (Although, we should acknowledge that perhaps a reason more rich and powerful people seek out dommes is because they can afford to.) Yes, if you spend any time in New York's BDSM dungeons, you're likely to run into a lot of Hasidic Jews. Stereotypes are often rooted in reality. But those stereotypes only scratch the surface of what BDSM is about.

One of the biggest illusions about D/s relationships is the dominant partner is the one who has "the power." Not so much, actually. While the dominant is superficially in control, the sub is the one who ultimately calls the shots, because they're *agreeing* to be subservient. The domme is the one who's responsible for keeping the sub interested in the game, because as soon as the sub gets bored, the game's over. This, of course, is what makes BDSM *consensual* domination (otherwise you're legit just raping someone).

One of my favorite parts of the job was getting a glimpse into the more unique and extreme fantasies that clients would come to Daisy with. Whips and chains are just the tip of the iceberg. For example, a common request from clients was "breath play," which includes choking, smothering, and face-sitting. Face-sitting is when you sit on a guy's face and smother him with your ass. It's also called "queening" because when you do it you look like a queen sitting on a human throne (glamorous). Infantilization was a big request, which involves putting a guy in diapers and spanking him and pretending to breast-feed him and yelling at him when he pees his pants, et cetera. Animal transformation is also pretty trendy, which is essentially making a guy act like a dog or a cow or whatever. Another big fantasy for subs is to feel owned. On multiple occasions I watched Daisy pretend to purchase a man from a fake "catalog of slaves" (in reality, a Macy's catalog).

One of the most common requests that Daisy got from clients was "forced-bi," which, as I mentioned earlier, is forcing a straight dude to suck cock. Daisy was famous for her forced-bi scenes because she was able to produce multiple "studs" at the drop of a hat. Studs are guys who come in on sessions for free and get their dicks sucked by the subs. And Daisy's studs typically weren't gay—they tended to be straight, bi-curious, or heteroflexible, and wanted to be a stud either for kicks or because they loved Daisy and wanted to serve her. It was amazing how many men Daisy had on call, who would serve her simply for the pleasure of it. These types of subs are often called "lifestyle slaves"—men whose fantasy is to continually service a woman, but who don't necessarily pay to do a proper BDSM session with her. They're unpaid interns, basically. Daisy's many lifestyle slaves would do everything from driving her to the airport, to taking out her air conditioner, to writing her emails. Her most devoted intern had been on call for her 24/7 for years, lived his life in a chastity belt that only she had the key to, and slept with his phone on just in case she called needing something. Now, whenever I find myself thinking *My life is kinda weird*, I remind myself about that guy.

Sometimes Daisy's clients called on her to help act out the sexual abuse they'd experienced as children. While she sometimes found it a little disturbing, if she felt it could help them recover from an experience, then she was all for it. This is not uncommon. For *some* people, BDSM is about reenacting trauma from your childhood, but in a controlled environment, which becomes a form of therapy. Daisy would often talk about how BDSM was actually very therapeutic for her, too, which in turn made her understanding and compassionate with people who came to her to work through their issues.

A couple of years ago, I interviewed Bobbi Starr, a porn star who has done a lot of kink and fetish work with the porn site Kink.com. Bobbi told me: "I have friends who do pro-domme sessions that say the job is one third dominatrix, one third business, and one third therapist. People will walk into their dungeon and say, 'I have this and this going on in my life, and I need you to beat it out of me.'" This could not be more true to my experience. In almost every session with Daisy, the submissive would have a moment of catharsis in which they would speak unedited about their life, fears, and fantasies. It was clear that Daisy was seeing a part of these people that wasn't seen by the rest of the world. It's rare to witness such radical honesty. It always felt like a special and privileged experience to watch someone in such a vulnerable state. In other words, the domme is not just the person with the whip, she's also an escape. Maybe God *is* a babe in latex after all.

For a lot of people, BDSM is about getting outside of yourself, and when it's good, it can be an out-of-body experience. Often, for a submissive, this moment of transcendence is known as "subspace." Subspace is sort of like an orgasm for a BDSM sub. It's basically a very intense mental and/or emotional response to something of an extreme nature that's being done to you, whether you're being beaten, humiliated, pissed on, et cetera. Since subspace is different for everyone, it's a little ambiguous to describe. But I guess you could think of it as the BDSM equivalent of having a breakthrough moment in talk therapy. Like I once saw a guy completely break down into tears while being waterboarded by Daisy (yes, "sensual waterboarding" is a thing—Google it). And once they achieve subspace, usually all a sub can think about is getting back there.

In her enlightening book on sex-positive culture, *Real Live Nude Girl* (1997), Dr. Carol Queen, sociologist, sexologist, and self-described whore, writes about achieving subspace from her personal perspective as someone who craves pain. She describes masochism as being "a deeply embodied starving for something—pleasure, catharsis, self-knowledge, adrenaline and endorphins, intensity, altered physical and emotional states. There are other ways to get there: The way I bottom tends to send me on emotional, not necessarily physical, journeys, though it's always most intense when my sexual body is involved. The notion that masochists like pain mistakes, I think, a more complex reality: They like the places pain can take them."

I think a lot of people hear these stories and think, *What the fuck is wrong with these people?* And I get it. I'm not a saint, either. I admit that on more than one occasion I found myself thinking, *These people are freaks. And worse, freaks with bad style.* But as time went by, and I became closer with certain people in the BDSM scene, I grew to admire in people some of the same qualities that I was judgmental of in the beginning. Ultimately, I came to respect people who weren't ashamed of what they wanted sexually and who had the confidence to go out and get it, even if it was something that most people would consider gross or embarrassing. I respected their embracing of taboo pleasures and seeking of a community of like-minded pervs with whom to share the intimate parts of their lives—their fantasies, their orgasms, their vulnerabilities, even their *mucus*. That takes a lot of guts. I mean, most people can't even muster up the courage to talk to someone in a bar. And if paying a random girl from the internet to abduct and torture you enables you to be a better, more sane human being, then who am I to judge?

Honestly, I can relate to the paradoxical motivations of many of the masochists I met back in my dungeon days. The term "masochism," coined in the nineteenth century, was named after Leopold von Sacher-Masoch, an Austrian novelist who is best known for the infamous novella *Venus in Furs* (1870), in which he wrote about his own fantasies and fetishes, especially for dominant women wearing fur. In her book *Lesbian Choices* (1995), Claudia Card writes: "In Sacher-Masoch's novels, the masochist is a man who seeks, receives and enjoys punishment and humiliation from a woman who willingly dishes them out; the man becomes ever more attracted to her as a result. This is paradoxical. Masochism, unlike sadism, sounds like a self-contradictory concept: how can one enjoy one's own pain or suffering if one's pain or suffering is, by definition, a sensation or other experience that one does not enjoy? How can one want to suffer, if suffering is, by definition, not getting what one wants? That some apparently do want and enjoy it is the paradox of masochism."

While all this BDSM exploration was unfolding in my life, I was still in a relationship with Max. Although our relationship started off pretty normal, in hindsight—and through therapy and an array of embarrassing self-discovery techniques—I can admit that I was in an abusive relationship. I had a boyfriend who would constantly put me down, who would call me stupid, tell me I was fat, tell me my writing sucked, tell me I was "aging badly" (lol, I was twenty-five)...basically every cliché of what you could say to a person to make them feel like shit. And bizarrely, I took it. And even more bizarrely, the more he insulted me, the more I wanted his approval. I felt that if I could just be a bit more successful, more eloquent at a dinner party, skinnier, *whatever*, he would finally be like, "Wow, you *are* amazing—I never noticed!" I fed on the rare moments of affection from him, and clung to them in the darkest times. And so I can empathize with the masochistic motivation that, despite all the pain, you keep coming back, until at a point, you almost crave the pain, because at least the person you care about is paying attention to you. I can relate to wanting to be out of control.

I know our relationship sounds horrible and unhealthy, but in an attempt at my defense and to understand the masochist, I think a lot of relationships cycle in and out of similar power dynamics (although, hopefully to a lesser degree). It's rare for a relationship to be evenly balanced. All relationships have a power structure, and it's usually clear who has the reins. In some, the power dynamic is more subtle, a constant ebb and flow of leverage. In others, the scales are not so even. Usually, at any given time, one partner is more into the other, in turn giving the desired "the power," and turning the desirer into a needy, submissive mess who's eager to please. This, clearly, turns the desired off (there's literally nothing less attractive than someone doing exactly what you want, right?), which results in the desirer becoming even more desperate. Until, that is, the desirer hits a breaking point, and is like, "Peace, I can't take this anymore." This then obviously triggers the desired to be like, "No, don't go!" and thus the power balance evens out again. Rinse and repeat ad nauseum.

Basically, anyone who believes that sex is a peaceful expression of love is ill informed. Sex is primal. It's hunting. It's aggression. It's a constant struggle for control. It's about testing boundaries and regressing to a more animal state. We can look at sadomasochism as just being a more intense, more intentional, and ideally more therapeutic version of that (except with more latex).

Thankfully, I eventually got to a place with Max where I couldn't take it anymore. Like I said earlier: The sub is the one who ultimately calls the shots, because as soon as they're over it, the game no longer exists. The difference between our relationship and a consensual BDSM relationship, however, is that while I tolerated the pain, I hadn't explicitly asked for it. And that is the heart of what separates an abusive relationship from a kinky one. What I think is largely missing from the mainstream conversation around BDSM is that, at their core, these practices are about love, trust, respect, and mutual enjoyment.

BDSM isn't about ropes or whips—it's about using the power structures that are inherent in our lives, relationships, careers, and fantasies, and supercharging them in a controlled environment, to reach a state that's somewhere between God and an orgasm.

amoral tale
chapter 4

good girl, bad influence (and vice versa)

*I*t *all started so innocently…*
I awoke one hungover morning, reluctantly opened my eyes, and dragged my overheated laptop back to its home on my chest. Like I do every morning. It was a strange period: Max and I had just broken up. I'd just quit working with Daisy after nearly getting myself killed, and that was a huge cut to my income. Essentially, I was jobless, single, and broke, and dangerously close to my twenty-seventh birthday, which was one that felt significant to me. Twenty-seven, I told myself, was truly adult. It's the age at which you can no longer use inexperience and youthful stupidity as excuses for being bad at life. It was the age at which my mother gave birth to me, for Christ's sake. And what did I have to show for myself, other than a box full of jizz-soaked dog collars and a moderately impressive but not yet monetized online following of aspiring sluts?

That morning, like every morning, I opened my *Slutever* email account to see what epistolary gems I'd received during the night. Generally, this address is made use of exclusively by trolls, who send me emails with such poetic subject lines as "Why u b such a whore?" and "Yet another uninspiring female who 'writes' (with her tits)." And then occasionally I'll get an email from a confused nineteen-year-old girl that almost always includes one of the following two questions: "I can't come during sex—is my vagina broken?!" or "Does shaving my pussy make me a bad feminist?" (Answers: "Probably not" and "I hope not.") But this day was different. There, in my inbox, was an email with the intriguing subject line "help a hooker out." It read as follows:

So, straight to the point. I'm a call girl. Not full time, full time. But it's my livelihood, and I do it because I like it. It's an adrenaline rush, an ego rub-down, and a lot more interesting than data entry. But at the same time, it's kind of ostracizing. My parents know, and are more or less cool with it (I pay their rent too), but it's made any hope of a relationship kind of sticky. I meet cool guys, but never know when to drop the bomb on them. Is it weird if I'm in the bar and he goes "So what do you do?" and I'm like "Fuck strangers and sell my tampons, mostly"? Do I go all vague and mysterious, and tell him once I really like him? Do I tell him before I sleep with him? What's the ideal protocol? I'm too lazy to do the whole double-life thing, and I kind of miss falling asleep next to someone I like.

In my years of giving out questionable advice to internet randoms, I'd never been asked this. I was stumped by what felt like a deeply nuanced moral dilemma. I mulled it over for a few minutes, then responded: *I'm sorry, I have no idea how to help you. But do you want to get lunch?*

Her name was Madeline. As it turned out, she lived only three blocks from me, which felt like a sign of…something. She was the sort of woman who, when she walked into a restaurant, people looked up from their kale salads to gawk at: a five-foot-nine double-D bombshell with platinum-blond hair (natural) and the sort of happily oblivious smile specific to someone who grew up in California. She was a beautiful perversion of the American dream: a working class girl who, through sheer sexual power, had transformed herself into a multilingual, world-traveling badass (with a Céline bag)—and she was just twenty-three. I was instantly in awe of her. Over Nicoise salads, on that first blind friend date, Madeline told me the story of how she got into sex work.

Madeline grew up in Southern California, with on-and-off junkie parents who struggled to keep food in the fridge, making her own stale pizza bagels for dinner, taking it upon herself to raise her little brother, reading romance novels from Rite Aid while her parents drank cheap whiskey in lawn chairs—ya know, the classic white-trash American upbringing. (Well, minus the part where her parents got clean and joined a religious cult of hippies who followed Orthodox Jewish law despite not actually being Jewish, but whatever, minor detail.) As a senior in high school, Madeline knew she had to get the fuck out of Dodge, so she spent hours online in her school library, searching for a job as an au pair. Eventually, she found a family in some middle-of-nowhere town in Italy who were looking for a live-in nanny for the summer, one who could give their children English lessons in exchange for room and board and a small salary. She flew out the week after high school graduation.

Over the next couple of years, Madeline country-hopped around Europe, learning languages while working as a nanny for various families. Until one day, while she was living in Paris, something unexpected happened. She was on her way to pick up the little boy she nannied from school, casually applying mascara in the rearview mirror while driving—as one does—when she crashed her host family's car into a lamppost. Whoops? She was fine, but the car was totaled. Madeline knew that her bosses—gay dads—had been struggling with money after one of them had recently been laid off. She wanted to help them pay for the damages but had no savings. And so, in a moment of desperation, she went on whatever the French equivalent of craigslist is, looking for some sort of odd job to make quick cash. And that's when she stumbled upon the ad: €500 for a "rendezvous" with a supposedly handsome thirty-two-year-old businessman. She thought, *Fuck it*.

She met the businessman at a basic hotel. He was nondescript, nice enough, and "most importantly, not fat," Madeline recalled. He poured her a drink, made some pleasant small talk, and then they had bland sex for like thirty minutes, and then she went home. Madeline said that maybe, if that first experience had been weird or scary or uncomfortable, she would have taken the €500 and gone back to her life as a nanny, disregarding her foray into hookerdom as a random one-off. But weirdly, not only was the experience of being a whore *not* traumatizing, it was actually verging on forgettable. The next day, she gave the €500 to the dads, admitting to them how she'd made the money (this is something you'll learn about Madeline— she's irrationally honest). The family took the money, but promptly fired her because they didn't want a ho raising their son. (It was hard enough on the kid having two gay dads, they explained, and adding a whore into the mix was crossing a line.) But it didn't matter, because Madeline didn't need them anymore. She was a hooker now.

Over the next six months, Madeline's life changed drastically. After some Google research, she found out about the popular sugar daddy website SeekingArrangement. (To state what is probably obvious today, sugar daddy sites connect rich guys with younger women, who in turn go on to form "arrangements" that range from genuine romance to "the girlfriend experience" to pay-by-the-hour sex meetings.) Madeline used SA to find bored bankers and lonely dads to have more of these rendezvous with. After a few months, she started talking to a sugar daddy who lived in New York, a finance guy in his midforties. He offered her a deal: Come visit me in New York, and if we like each other, I'll pay for you to move here and give you an allowance of $7,500 a month. Being the industrious twenty-year-old slut that she was, Madeline accepted the offer. Within a month she was living in her own studio apartment in Manhattan. She didn't know a single person in the city besides her sugar daddy, who she only saw a couple of times a week, for dinners and sex, but she had a disposable income, which she used to buy friends. "When you're twenty," Madeline told me, "all you have to do is buy people drinks, and they'll hang out with you. I felt so rich. I'd walk into dive bars in Williamsburg and buy everyone a shot, like a loser, but it worked. I felt like the twenty-year-old female equivalent of my clients: Essentially, we were both paying people to stand next to us. I love capitalism. It's so perverse!"

Her relationship with the finance guy lasted four months, at which point he told her that he wanted to start paying a different random girl from the internet to be his fake girlfriend. Madeline, being the airheaded twenty-year-old slut that she was, hadn't saved any money—she'd spent it all on mojitos for her fake friends—and needed a new way to pay her $2,350-a-month rent. So she went back on SA to look for another sugar daddy. This time, however, it was harder to find a guy willing to pay her in large monthly installments (the first guy, she realized, might have been beginner's luck). Desperate and with an overdrawn bank account, she decided to see multiple men at a time, even if they couldn't promise her more than a one-off. It was at this point that Madeline began thinking of "sugaring" as a business, rather than just a potentially problematic thing she did on the side for money while primarily focusing on "finding herself" or whatever. Having sex, she decided, would be her job. It didn't take her long to figure out that she was really fucking good at it.

To some, Madeline's story might sound remarkable—a fluke, an exception to the rule, maybe even a stroke of bizarre luck. But in reality, she's not that special.

Today, an increasing number of young people (primarily women) are using their bodies to make money. This might not sound so revolutionary—clearly, women have been subsidized by men in exchange for companionship since pretty much the dawn of time. (We used to call this dynamic "marriage," though now we call it "sex work"—but whatever, minor detail.) What's different is that today these so-called mutually beneficial relationships are facilitated online, through sugar daddy websites.

The sugar world is not a small subculture. These websites boast literally *millions* of subscribers, many of whom are women at top universities. As of 2016, more than 1.2 million American college students were signed up to the most popular sugar site, SeekingArrangement, and that number is growing rapidly. On average, 2,000 new students with an email account belonging to an American university sign up to the site every day. According to SA's 2016 membership data, 1,486 students were registered to SeekingArrangement at New York University alone. But of course, not all members are students. In 2016, SeekingArrangement reported having 5.5 million members worldwide, and 3.25 million members active in the United States. Here's a crazy statistic: Approximately 2 percent of adult females in the

U.S. are sugar babies. It's funny to think that 2 percent is also the estimated percentage of gay people in America. And yet, no one cares about sex workers' rights.

The sugar phenomenon has been reported on everywhere from the *Wall Street Journal* to CNN to *Vanity Fair* to the BBC. Most reports have cited the increasing burden of college tuition as a primary catalyst (on average, American students today graduate $35,000 in debt). Others say it's the result of wealth inequality, and the crushing cost of cities like New York, L.A., and San Francisco for young people. Others blame the websites themselves, for making these types of arrangements easier than ever to find. To me, the most interesting stimulus of sugar culture (as well as other forms of consensual sex work) is the radical sexual freedom of today's young woman, who fucks who she wants, and might as well get paid for it, too.

In essence, sugaring is a modern, increasingly visible form of prostitution, which has been dressed up and repackaged in such a way that it's become nearly socially acceptable (key word being "nearly"). Some sugar babies don't consider themselves sex workers at all, feeling that sugar arrangements fall into a gray area, as opposed to clearly transactional, pay-by-the-hour sex. Other women are happy to interchange the term "sugar baby" with "prostitute." When asked why they sugar, many women will reply with some version of: "I have a lot of sex anyway—why not get paid for it?" Or "Why would I work at a coffee shop for ten dollars an hour when I could make eight hundred dollars to sleep with a banker who's not even that bad?" Many women have reported in magazine interviews and documentaries, on social media and elsewhere how being a sugar baby has enabled them to travel, support an artistic career, pay for higher education, buy beautiful clothing, eat at fancy restaurants, and basically avoid living in a cockroach-filled converted loft in Ridgewood with seven roommates who all create awful performance art. If you ask me, I'd rather suck the 1 percent's dick than watch someone make art with their period any day.

But back to Madeline. After that first enlightening lunch, she and I became fast friends. I just loved listening to her talk—we'd meet for drinks or take long walks along the East River, and I'd record her with my phone while she told all her best whore stories—like the time she helped a disabled guy lose $30,000 in Vegas, or the time when she blew an eighty-year-old man who was hooked up to an oxygen tank. It all sounded so glamorous. But aside from the entertainment factor, what amazed me about Madeline was how openly she talked about sex work. The cheerful, casual nature with which she discussed hooking made you forget that anyone would consider her lifestyle shameful or taboo. Instead, it just seemed really, well…practical.

At the time we met, I was sleeping on a gross futon mattress pad in a curtained-off section of a lesbian's living room. While I was grateful that the rent was super cheap, this was obviously not the ideal living situation. But a few months into our friendship, Madeline's roommate moved out of their converted loft apartment. The room had no windows and was basically a dank cave made out of scrap wood, but at least it had walls (the bar was pretty low for me at that point). And so, Madeline and I officially became roomies.

The first weekend that we lived together, Madeline flew to Paris to bang a Saudi prince. Obviously. He flew her first-class and booked her a room in a five-star hotel. They had only communicated via email at this point, and had never even spoken on the phone. I'd always ask Madeline if she was worried that one of these guys was going to go all Gary Ridgway on her, but she would always just shrug it off, saying she felt safer meeting someone through a website—specifically, one that requires a monthly credit card fee—than she did picking up a random guy at a bar. "People just don't get killed at fancy hotels," she'd say with a smile.

When she arrived at her Paris hotel room, there were four dozen roses on the bed, next to a bottle of Dom Perignon from her birth year. I got a text from her that evening: *I love him! He gave me $5,000! And he looks exactly like Aladdin!* The text came in while I was working a shift at the crappy Chinese restaurant where I waitressed, and for a second I seriously considered walking out of the restaurant and into oncoming traffic.

About a month or so into our cohabitation, I was lying on Madeline's bed, watching her cut up a kitchen sponge and insert a piece of it into the depths of her vagina—a little DIY hooker trick that allows you to have sex while sneakily on your period. She was getting ready for lunch with one of her SDs—a fiftyish businessman and ex-CIA agent named Edward. He was "a genius," according to Madeline (although this is how she describes almost everyone she meets). Edward had been married three times, and following his second divorce, he promised himself that from then on, he would only cheat on his wife with multiple women at a time. The reason for this, he told Madeline, was that he's a hopeless romantic. If he's alone with a woman, he can't help but fall head over heels in love with her. So to prevent that from happening, he now only had extramarital sex in threesomes or more. "It makes sense, when you think about it," Madeline said with a shrug. She was chugging a Diet Coke and plucking her eyebrows, her pupils dilated to the appropriate size for someone on 20 mg of Adderall. "You should come with me next time," she said. "I'm sure he'd love to meet you."

It was a bizarre moment. I'd been watching Madeline's life admiringly for months; I'd been both fascinated and turned on by her stories; I had worked as a dominatrix; I was by anyone's standards a dedicated slut in my personal life. And yet, in complete honesty, I'd never thought to myself, *I should just become a hooker.* As soon as she said it, I was actually annoyed that I hadn't thought of it myself.

One week later I was riding the 6 train uptown on my way to my first professional threesome. Madeline had helped me pick out my outfit, vetoing most of my wardrobe for being "too hipster." Apparently my chunky platforms, meticulously smudged eyeliner, and semi-ironic mock-lace Rainbow skankwear were not the right look. "This is not the moment to subvert the male gaze or to fight the patriarchy or whatever," Madeline told me, rolling her eyes. "If you're going to do this, you have to appeal to a standard of beauty that the most basic, white-bread, man-baby finance bro finds attractive." This became a sentiment that Madeline repeated to me many, many times over the coming months. At first it kind of weirded me out, because I'd never seen myself as someone who was trying to subvert any gazes—sure, there was a somewhat satirical element to the way I dressed ("Elle Woods at an art school gang bang" was my style reference), but I still certainly looked feminine and—at least in my mind—attractive in a way that wasn't actively fighting any social norms of beauty. Also, I was incredulous that *all* rich guys only wanted to see women wearing Louboutins and a push-up bra. Surely beauty is subjective, even when it comes to the 1 percent, right? "No," Madeline insisted. And so I gave in and let her dress me up like a horny senator's wife.

On the subway, Madeline briefed me on what was about to go down. She said her meetings with Edward generally followed a similar pattern. He invited her for lunch at a nice restaurant in Midtown. He would be seated at the table waiting for her when she arrived, smiling too hard, wearing a suit, and sipping vodka on the rocks. Another woman always appeared at these lunches, invited by Edward, and Madeline usually didn't know anything about her until she arrived. These women were generally smart—"in law school or something"—and pretty, but not "obnoxiously pretty." Together they would eat a nice meal and have a couple of drinks, and afterward Edward would walk them to a nearby hotel, one girl on each arm, and they'd go up to his room and fuck. Each girl left with $1,000. It seemed easy enough. In the week leading up to this, the thing that had weirded me out the most was that we were meeting at 12:30 p.m.—oppressively early for a threesome, in my opinion. However, Madeline seemed unfazed by it. She said she preferred to meet SA guys in the daytime, because it left her evenings free to fuck guys from OkCupid. Naturally.

By the time we got off the train at Grand Central, I was so nervous that I became genuinely worried I might have a panic attack. But I didn't really understand *why* I was freaking out. Threesomes were nothing new to me—I'd even had one with Madeline, actually—so that certainly wasn't the source of my anxiety. I'd also slept with multiple men in their forties and fifties, so the older man thing wasn't the issue, either. And, like anyone who's ever gone home with someone they met in a bar, I had no moral qualms about fucking someone I barely knew. In fact, I'd actually been in a very similar situation to this only a few months before. A friend of mine, who's in an open marriage, had invited me over "for drinks" with her and her husband, who I'd never met. I'd understood what was unspoken in that invitation, and while taking the train to her Upper East Side apartment, I was well aware that I was on my way to bang both my friend and a man who I knew almost nothing about. And sure, I was sort of nervous on that train ride, too. But that was more of an excited nervousness. This time, I was breaking out in a rash.

There was no other way to look at it: The only thing that separated this situation from the many others like it in my lifetime was the money. So what was it about getting paid that changed the vibe so much? Was it about expectation—feeling like because I was being compensated I had to look a certain way, act a certain way, be more agreeable, fuck more generously, laugh louder, come harder? I posed these concerns to Madeline. "You can just laugh at your regular volume," she said, only half paying attention to me, mainly trying to stay upright in her four-inch stilettos. "But maybe," she reconsidered, "if you can't actually come, you should fake it…for good measure."

"Don't worry, I'm good at that," I assured her.

"But just so you know," she said, "I would never fake it with a guy who wasn't paying me. They just don't deserve it." Good advice.

Just as Madeline said, Edward was waiting for us with a smile. He wasn't bad-looking—fiftyish, Latino, in shape, teeth a couple of shades too white. I wouldn't go out of my way to talk to him in a bar, but I've fucked worse. He told us that he could hang out for exactly two hours, because he was sleeping on the Da Vinci rhythm and 2:30 p.m. was his nap time.

"What's the Da Vinci rhythm?" I asked, practically chugging my martini.

"It's an alternative sleep pattern," he explained. "You sleep for fifteen minutes every three or four hours."

"Sounds dangerous," I said.

"I suppose I live dangerously," he said with a shrug. I couldn't tell if he was being sarcastic.

"So Madeline tells me you only have threesomes."

"It's true." He nodded. "Out of respect for my wife."

Over the course of the meal I learned that Edward was born in Mexico to a Mexican mother and American father. He grew up poor. He really wanted me to know this—he had been poor, *very poor*, as a child, which apparently gave him free rein to act as decadently as he liked in his middle age without guilt. When he was fifteen his family had moved to Nevada. He'd been a smart kid, and by eighteen he'd made half a million dollars gambling, counting cards in Vegas. He went to Yale. After college he got a job at the CIA. He lived for five years in China, working as a spy, then decided he wasn't cut out for the job and quit. He started a business and then sold it for a bunch of money. After that he started another one and sold it for even more money. By his midforties he'd made enough that he could devote the rest of his life to having almost daily threesomes with random women from the internet at awkward intervals throughout the day in accordance with his weird nap schedule.

I have to admit, I was reluctantly impressed by Edward's story. By this point, I was both drunk and intrigued enough that my rash had subsided. I was actually having a really fun time. Madeline, on the other hand, was immersed in her phone, clearly having heard this sermon like twenty times already.

Edward told me that one of the first things they teach you in the CIA is how to lie. I immediately grabbed a pen and a napkin. While I took notes, he explained that a good lie has three main components: First, you should keep your lie as close to the truth as possible. Don't fabricate wild stories or excuses, because made-up stories are difficult to remember, and they're even harder to back up if you get caught. Second, don't give out unnecessary details—if someone asks you how your night went, tell him, "It was good," and leave it at that. You should never give people information they don't need, because information is what gives you away. And third, it's important to remember that it's not just about *how* you lie, but also *who* you're lying to. Lying is a cooperative act. A lie has no power until someone believes it, and it's a lot easier to convince someone of a lie they *want* to be true. "'No, honey, I didn't cheat on you' is actually quite an easy lie to get away with," he said, grinning, "because your target wants to believe that you're telling the truth."

Maybe all of this sounds sort of obvious to you. But it didn't to me at the time. Or at least, breaking it down like that—presenting the act of lying as something skillful and mathematical, rather than moral—was exciting to me. In hindsight, it's so predictable that I'd go for a guy like Edward: an unquestionable sex maniac.

As soon as we got back to Edward's hotel, it was clear that he would be in total control of how this all went down. I was more than happy to sign over power of attorney. Luckily, Edward was a natural dictator—"Get on your knees," "Turn around," "No, not that way, this way." All we had to do was follow his instructions—it was so easy! I wasn't super physically attracted to him, but I tend to close my eyes during sex anyway, so whatever. The only awkward moment was when he kept insisting that Madeline put her fingers in my butt, and she kept being like, "No fucking way, I just got a gel manicure this morning." But other than that, it was totally chill. And I didn't even have to fake it, because I just made myself come while watching them fuck, like real-life porn.

And then came the part where he handed me $1,000. Now, this is the funny thing about being offered money in exchange for sex: It seems like such a deviant and far-fetched idea...until it actually happens, at which point it suddenly seems extremely logical. It's like, "You're going to pay me money to have sex? Only an idiot would turn that down." Or like how in middle school your friends were like, "Ugggh, how much would you have to be paid to fuck Mr. Shepard?!" And you were all "EWW!!!! Three *million* dollars!" But that's just because you'd never paid rent before, and then you grow up and realize that realistically it's more like three hundred.

In the elevator, on our way back down to earth, I felt a new sense of power with the money shoved down my bra (he'd put it into my handbag, but I relocated it to my bra because that felt more cinematic). "Threesomes are *the best*," Madeline cooed. "You only have to do half the work, and they last half as long, because the guy can't control himself." She was such a savvy businesswoman. "I've been thinking," she said, half seriously. "Andy Warhol said making money is art, so if we make money by having sex, does that mean when we have sex, we're making art?" I didn't have an answer. "One time," she added, "I got my period while with a client, and afterward the sheets looked like a Pollock canvas."

professional baby

The day after our threesome, I quit my job at the Chinese restaurant—literally the following day. A premature ejaculation, in hindsight. But when you realize that you can make a grand in just two hours of "work," it seems ridiculous to keep a waitressing job that pays you the same amount for two solid weeks of physical and psychological torture. It's like Woody Allen said in *Deconstructing Harry*: "Every hooker I ever speak to tells me that it beats the hell out of waitressing."

It was just weeks before my twenty-seventh birthday. I'd been working at the Chinese place part-time for almost two years, and it was really starting to wear on me. On some days, I felt like my life and writing career were going pretty okay—*Slutever*'s readership was growing, I was writing cover stories for *Dazed & Confused* magazine, and I was making a satirical sex-ed web series for *Vice*. But none of those things paid me any real fucking money. It was unnerving to think that, to date, my most lucrative output had been my urine. *Slutever* brought in literally zero dollars, and *Vice* was still in a phase where they insisted the company was doing *you* a favor by giving you a platform and making you "cool." (If only you could pay your rent in cultural cachet!) *Dazed* paid me roughly $350 for a cover feature that took me a week to write. Basically, the publishing industry was and is a fucking nightmare, and despite working really hard, I was well below the poverty line and totally unable to support myself.

And while I was proud of the creative work I was doing, I couldn't help but feel like my waitressing job was representative of my failure as a writer. (And it didn't help that once every couple of weeks, a customer would come in and be like, "Oh my god, I love your blog!" and I'd smile and then have to get down on my knees to wipe up soy sauce from beneath their clogs.)

Like being a dominatrix, sugaring felt like a way that I could make money fast, so rather than devoting thirty hours a week to being a noodle slave, I could spend more time on MY ART (bleh). But sugar-babying seemed even better than being a dominatrix, because it paid more, and because I enjoy having sex exponentially more than I enjoy peeing into strange men's mouths.

However, as soon as I quit the restaurant I regretted it, because I realized that I was kind of freaked out. Having a paid threesome with a man your friend vetted for you was one thing, but creating my own escort profile and going it alone felt scary. And more than being scared of the logistics of selling sex, what I was really scared of was the idea of becoming a Sex Worker—with a capital *S W*. What did that say about me? Who was I? No little girl grows up with the dream of becoming a prostitute (although if that girl exists, I definitely want to meet her). No matter how much of an enlightened, sex-radical feminist you grow up to be, the moment you make the decision to become a hooker, you can't help but wonder—what did I do wrong to end up here?

There are many reasons why I—or someone in my

position—would think this way. The most obvious is that, almost unanimously, sex workers are thought to be gross, desperate skanks. And unfortunately, I didn't have many examples to aspire to of powerful, creative, respected women who also did sex work. I can't think of a single instance of a whore being portrayed in a positive light in a film or on TV. *Pretty Woman sort of* goes there, but the reason we're given permission to like Julia Roberts's character in the film is because she's a hooker who wants to be saved. Particularly, she wants to be saved by a rich white man who rescues her from her life of streetwalking victimhood and engages her in a classist civilizing process, ending with her being dressed up in Chanel. It's the classic rags-to-riches story, ending with all parties segueing happily into social convention.

But almost ubiquitously, whores are thought to be tragic. It's no coincidence that "You're a whore" is one of the most popular insults flung at women—by men, but also by other women. This is in part because of the lingering belief that women should be pure, that women who have a lot of sex are somehow worth less than those who don't. And even if you're intelligent enough not to believe that bullshit, that doesn't mean that you don't still want to be accepted—by your friends, by your family, by society. The reason people get married when they're not really ready is basically the same reason that people don't become sex workers when they kinda want to—you know what I mean? It's because they don't want to be ostracized. You can rationalize that sex workers should be given an equal amount of respect as any other person while simultaneously understanding that, in the world we live in, that's unlikely to be the case.

This stigma around sex work exists even in the most liberal and ostensibly sex-positive circles. It's highly unlikely that today, even at, let's say, a dinner of intellectuals in New York City, a woman could come out as an escort and have anyone consider that a "good job"—even if she earned more than everyone else at the table. It's sort of funny, because when you really break it down, getting paid to have sex sounds like a pretty good deal, right?

For decades, the cultural conversation around sex work has been essentially the same: Sex workers are abused, dehumanized victims, and sex work is bad for society. In the 1970s, radical feminists and antiporn crusaders like Andrea Dworkin and Catharine MacKinnon made it their mission to perpetuate the cultural misconception that all sex work is inherently degrading, bolstering both the sexual objectification of women and the patriarchy. Some have gone as far as to say that all sex work is rape. We don't consider consensual sex violence, and we don't consider being paid violence, but if you put the two together, you're being exploited and need to be saved…apparently. While the moralists who preach this ostensibly mean well, what this discourse does is imply that sex workers have no agency. Even if a sex worker insists that she works of her own free will, she shouldn't be taken seriously, because she must be either lying or brainwashed or on crack.

So, of course, when faced with my own decision about

whether to begin escorting, all these things were swirling around in my mind—along with "What the fuck would I do if my Catholic parents ever found out?" Of course, I had a choice. I was in no way being forced into selling my body in the dark and sensational way that we often imagine is the case with sex workers. I wouldn't have starved or become homeless or died if I didn't set up a sugar baby profile. But I might have had to move out of New York. And I might have had to give up on my dream of being a writer, perhaps taking out a loan to go back to school, choosing instead a career that was more practical but less fulfilling. And I didn't want to do those things. So I made what I felt was the best choice for me at the time. I looked at myself in the mirror and said: "Yo, you have sex with people you don't like all the time; you might as well get fucking paid for it."

Madeline, ever the mentor, offered to help me make my SeekingArrangement profile. I remember that afternoon vividly: We were lying on the living room couch in our pajamas, scarfing gummy bears, as Madeline casually spouted bits of hooker wisdom. "Okay, so the most important thing to remember when filling out your profile is that men have small brains but *huge* egos," she said, mouth full of candy. "You have to convince these guys that they're *taking care* of you, rather than paying for you, because that makes them feel pathetic. You want to make them feel powerful by using words like 'benefactor' and 'mentor.' Basically, you're a scared baby lamb in the big city who needs a real man with a big cock and a big fat wallet to show you the way—or you'll die." It was all so…predictable.

Madeline explained that there's generally two types of guys on these sites. She'd nicknamed them the Bleeding Hearts and the Contract Sugar Daddies. A Bleeding Heart actually thinks he's in a relationship with you—he wants to put his hand on your inner thigh in public, to go to sporting events together, and for you to pretend to come like five times during sex, basically. Bleeding Hearts are often saying things like "I'm always really generous with my girlfriends, so I don't see why this is any different." When the issue of money comes up, you both have to pretend that it's for your rent, or a camera that will help you launch your photography career, or basically anything to distract from the fact that he has to pay a girl to stand next to him. And then there's the Contract Sugar Daddies. These guys are more businesslike about it—they pay you a set fee each time they see you, or give you an allowance each month. These guys, she explained, tend to be more confident—they're not embarrassed about the money element of the relationship, meaning they generally see sugar relationships as a convenience rather than as a necessity. Maybe they're simply too busy or lazy to date for real, or maybe they're married. The married guys, she explained, are the best, because they tend to have the least amount of free time to hang out with you.

Madeline prepared me pretty well, but being the good journalist that I am, I wanted to do my own research. So I set up roughly a million dates. Essentially, SA functions like any other dating site: Everyone fills out a profile explaining who they are and what they're looking for. The main difference is that, on SA, men's profiles list their net worth, yearly income, and an estimate of how much they're willing to spend on a sugar baby (ranging from a "practical" amount of $1,000 to $3,000 a month to a "high" amount of over $10,000 a month). There's also a box where they note their relationship status—the "married but looking" option is one I assume they don't offer on most "normal" dating sites.

At first, I wasn't being selective, and I agreed to meet pretty much every guy who sent me a message. This proved to be a huge mistake and a nightmarish waste of time. I mean, imagine applying the same logic to Tinder—literally terrifying. In my defense, it's harder to assess who you're meeting through SA, because the majority of men don't upload photos, for purposes of discretion, so you're left assessing them by whatever they write in their profile. But they all write the same fucking thing. I'm paraphrasing, but it goes something like:

Handsome businessman looking for beautiful young woman to explore the world with. I'm very busy and travel too much to have a regular relationship. I don't mean to brag, but I know quite a bit about art and fine wines. Travel junkie!! Chemistry a must. No professionals!!

Translated into reality, that means:

Aging, frumpy businessman looking for someone young to have sex with because my wife won't fuck me anymore. I sometimes go to Florida on vacation. I like drinking and traveling, like everyone else on earth, and I've heard of Damien Hirst. I don't want to pay you by the hour and you have to pretend to like me.

Of course, I didn't know all this at the time. I was a newbie. But I was about to embark on what I now reflect on as my second desensitization period.

The first guy I met was Jack. He was thirty-five and referred to himself on his profile as a "Cary Grant type." We met at a dive bar in the West Village, and it turned out he looked less like a 1930s movie star and more like the Unabomber. When I asked him what he did for a living, he told me he was a "student of the world." It didn't sound very lucrative. To make a short story even shorter, it turned out that Jack lived in his mom's basement in Long Island, and had recently been given control of his parents' bank account, following his father's death. I told him I had to pee and snuck out the back entrance.

The next guy was a chubby-faced bond trader who, about seven minutes into our meeting, asked me if I wanted to move with him to Fort Lauderdale. After him was the guy from the Texan oil family, who took me for drinks at the Peninsula hotel and told me I looked like a "perfect little Nazi." There was more than one guy who didn't even show up, and multiple men who, when I brought up the financial component, tried to make me feel embarrassed about asking for money in exchange for my time—as if that weren't the exact fucking dynamic that the site was founded on. As it turned out, they don't call it sex *work* for nothing—and I hadn't even banged anyone yet. I felt like I was going on a million tiny job interviews and never being hired. These were not the glamorous rendezvous I'd had in mind.

meeting my $oul mate

I had a good feeling about this guy. He had invited me for lunch at Milos, a Greek place in Midtown with a distinct expense-account vibe, which seemed like a good sign. I excitedly put on my new prostitute costume. (In an effort to take the babying business more seriously, I'd Googled "Where do prostitutes shop?" and the most highly rated response on Yahoo Answers was Zara, so I went there and bought a Dolce & Gabbana knock-off dress that felt like the perfect combo of class and trash.) I was feeling very powerful.

He was a geeky guy, around forty, with awkwardly long limbs and thick glasses resting on a big nose. The sort of guy who could put on a $10,000 suit and it would still be obvious that he'd been beaten up on the daily in high school (aka my type). He asked me questions about where I grew up and about my writing, which no other guy from the site had done (I'm pretty sure they all assumed I did nothing). And then I asked him what he did for a living, and that's when my stomach made a leap for my throat, because I suddenly felt like he might just be *the one* (a different *one* than the one we usually talk about, but you know what I mean).

I can't give away too much information about him or I'll get sued, but let's just say he created an app that you almost definitely have downloaded at some point. I knew I needed to make a really good impression, so I downed three glasses of wine in like fifteen minutes. While I was drowning my nerves, App Guy was aggressively ordering more and more food, sending roughly every third dish back to the kitchen. "You have to send something back, or they don't take you seriously," he informed me with a straight face. When I brought up the arrangement, he abruptly cut me off. "Talking about money is boring," he said, waving his hand in front of my face as if to say *shut the fuck up*. "How much do you want? You want two grand? I'll give you two grand. Let's just get drunk." That was easier than I'd expected.

He ordered me drink after drink, insisting that we were "celebrating," but kept refusing to say what exactly this celebration was for. I thought it was *slightly* odd that he seemed so intent on getting wasted—it was barely noon, after all—but an alcoholic loves an enabler, and so I chose to ignore what in hindsight was clearly a red flag.

By the time we got back to the St. Regis, where he was staying, I was more than tipsy. I made my best effort to remain upright as I stumbled through the lobby and into the elevator. Soon we were on his bed making out—sort of. We'd kiss for like five seconds, but then he'd find some ADD reason to get up and do something on the other side of the room—change the music, turn off the lights, close the curtain, turn the lights back on again. Eventually I got up and dragged him back to the bed by the arm, but then he just started awkwardly rubbing his face back and forth across my boobs, over my dress, with a blank expression on his face, as if he was meditating with his eyes open. It felt like that awkward scene in *Big* where Tom Hanks, who's secretly a thirteen-year-old boy in a man's body, is attempting to have sex with a woman while hiding the fact that he clearly has no idea what sex is. I suddenly felt like I was babysitting, and not in a hot way. I wanted to move things along, so I went for his zipper, but he dodged me and jumped up onto the bed. "This isn't right," he said. "It's the wrong moment. Let's go down to the bar and get another drink." And so I begrudgingly put on my heels as he dragged me by my wrist down to the bar.

The King Cole Bar at the St. Regis, with its opulent velvet armchairs and thirty-foot golden mural, is the sort of place you imagine Salvador Dalí sipping cocktails next to chic old ladies in Chanel. It's less the sort of place you go to take a drunken afternoon nap. But there I was, laid out on the velvet couch, my Zara dress riding up over my butt. App Guy was looking over the whiskey list. Their most expensive glass was $300. "Do you have anything better?" he asked the waiter, whose forced smile conveyed a quiet rage. "I only drink whiskey that's older than me. And I'm forty-two."

I put my hand on his inner thigh and slurred something along the lines of "Let's go back upstairs."

"I have a better idea," he said. "We should call up one of

your friends. Don't you have any hot friends who would come hang out with us?" *Predictable*, I thought. As a Millennial woman, I've grown to accept that first-date conversations tend to go something like this: Question 1: "Where are you from?" Question 2: "What do you do?" Question 3: "Do you have any hot friends who you might want to suck my dick with?" Sorry, but when did threesomes go from being a dessert to an appetizer?

I suggested Madeline, but he wasn't interested in her. "I don't want a *professional*," he said. "We need fresh blood." I told him that, unfortunately, I didn't have any friends who would be available to fuck a stranger at a moment's notice at 3 p.m. on a Wednesday, and that even if I did, I didn't know how I would explain this situation to them. He frowned and slumped back into the couch, letting out a long sigh of disappointment at the epic unfairness of life. I felt like a failed hooker.

And then I remembered my fan.

See, around this time I had this internet stalker fan-girl type person who'd been sending me near-daily Facebook messages with too many exclamation points. Ya know, like: "Hiiiii! I'm a student from Denmark!! I'm in New York for the summer on an internship!!!!! We should totally hang out because I've always felt like we could totally be best friends lolll!!!" Obviously, I never responded. But suddenly, Danish intern seemed newly appealing. "*Well…*" I said to App Guy, "I do have this one internet stalker who seems pretty desperate. She might be down."

He nodded excitedly. "She's perfect."

My Facebook message read: "Hi! Sorry I somehow missed your last 5 messages. But OMG I would totally love to hang! Actually do you want to come meet me and my boyfriend right now?" Followed by the sly-face emoji and the salsa-dancing-lady emoji. I had to type it with one eye closed, like a cartoon drunk person. She responded within two minutes. Overeager. She could be at the hotel in an hour. App Guy was thrilled. I was dizzy.

You know how's there's that tipping point when you're drinking, when you're trying to hold on to *just enough* sobriety to appear somewhat normal? And then there's that *other* tipping point when you're just straight-up trying to stay conscious? I was there. And then…I failed.

The next thing I remember, I was waking up with a dull headache in a dark, empty hotel room. Scary-ish, but also, realistically, not super foreign to me. The sky outside was dark, and since it was summer and the sun didn't set until around 8 p.m., I knew it had been at least five hours since my last memory. *Wait…was I just low-key raped?* I wondered while scraping dried drool off my face. I still had all my clothes on, so it seemed kosher. But my confusion quickly turned to anger: *Why the fuck did App Guy abandon me here? And more importantly, is he partying with my stalker without me?*

Quickly, without thinking, I got up and marched out of the room and down the hallway. I hadn't thought about where exactly I was going, but I was eager to get there. But about halfway down the hall I realized: *Oh shit, I'm not wearing any shoes. And I don't have my bag or my phone,*

*which I guess are back in the hotel room? And I don't have
a key to the room. And actually, now that I've walked down
the hall, I don't even remember what room number I came
out of. Fuck. I guess I could go to the front desk and ask for
help…looking like a crazy shoeless lost hooker. But actually,
I don't even know App Guy's last name. Uggghhh.*

For some reason—drunken rage logic—I decided to
pound my fist repeatedly on the door directly in front of
me. I think I wanted to use the phone? To call the front
desk? Honestly, I'm not entirely sure. But I was definitely
feeling confrontational and ready to yell at someone. And
then the door opened, and there stood a shirtless, very
sexy, and very confused-looking British man.

"…Hi?" said the shirtless man, who was roughly thirty
and had a nose that looked like it had been broken many
times over, but in a good way. He stared at me, waiting
for me to say something, but I just stood there with my
mouth open.

Him: "What's going on…?"

Me: "Oh, not much. What are you doing?"

Him: "Not much…"

Me: "Well, so, I'm staying at this hotel, and I happened
to misplace my key. Uh. And my shoes. And my phone.
Could I use yours?"

Once I was in his room I realized I really didn't want
to make that phone call, especially in front of the shirtless
hot British stranger. I was stalling. "So, what are you doing
in New York? What kind of business? Oh, really? I find finance so interesting."

He offered me some sparkling wine from the minibar. And then we started fucking, because I'm a slut (if you haven't figured that out already).

I'm sure the sex was fine, although not exceptional enough for me to remember the details. You could tell he worked out, though. Anyway, sometime after (or during?) the sex I fell asleep, and the next thing I knew I was being woken up by the British guy, far too politely. "Excuse me, miss, miss. Uh, I hate to wake you, but I was just thinking that you probably don't want to wake up here tomorrow without any of your things. Do you have somewhere to be?" He looked simultaneously scared for me and scared *of* me.

I looked at the clock: 11:30 p.m. Fuck. I grabbed the phone and called the front desk. "Um, hi, so, this is awkward, but I'm staying at this hotel with a friend and I seem to be lost. I think his name is—" The person on the other end interrupted me with a long, resentful sigh. "Yes," said the voice, "we've all been looking for you. Room 501." Whoops?

By the time I got my clothes back, the guys at the front desk had clearly informed App Guy of my whereabouts, because when I opened the door into the hallway there he was, staring at me, looking *sort of* amused but mainly like an angry schoolteacher.

"What were you doing in that room?"

"Oh, just…taking a nap."

He laughed a slow, maniacal laugh and placed his hand firmly on my lower back, leading me to his room. And there on his hotel bed was my fan, naked and touching herself. She was thin with tight brown curls and the bland, rectangular brown-framed glasses of a cartoon librarian. "So nice to finally meet you," I said, smiling awkwardly. She dropped her vibrator and ran over to hug me.

"I hope this is okay..." she said nervously.

"Hope what's okay?"

"Ya know, sleeping with your boyfriend. He said you wouldn't mind."

"Oh, he's not my..." And then I saw App Guy behind her, miming slitting his throat with his finger. I shut my mouth. "Anyway, sorry to arrive late to the party! So, where were we?" *And here we go again*, I thought.

We threesomed, which was fun and technically good but not necessarily what I was in the mood for at that precise moment. Throughout the whole thing, App Guy was repeatedly telling my fan how hot she was. "God, baby, you're gorgeous...fuck, it's so hot when you do that..." was the constant soundtrack. I kept arching my back, trying to get attention. At some point, she got up to go to the bathroom.

"I *love* fucking normal girls," App Guy whispered, swigging more whiskey. "They just want it so badly. We should do this more often—find really unspectacular girls and coax them back to our room." I was confused about whether I, too, was one of these unspectacular girls, but I figured that either way, this sounded like a better gig than being a noodle slave.

When it was finally over, App Guy pulled out a duffel

bag from the closet and unzipped it to reveal a ton of cash: impressive at first, until you looked closer and realized that it was mainly fives and ones. He started grabbing huge handfuls of bills and shoving them into our handbags without counting them. My fan looked confused.

"He's not exactly my boyfriend," I said, yawning aggressively. "Oh, and you're a prostitute now." I felt oddly proud of myself, like I was becoming Madeline. My fan seemed weirdly unfazed. Maybe because she's European? In a cab back to Brooklyn, she and I counted our money: it was $2,480, so $1,240 apiece. Not what I was promised, but I couldn't really complain, given that I fell unconscious and then left to fuck someone else for free in the middle of my shift. I've never been a very loyal employee.

This disaster threesome was the beginning of, well…I wouldn't necessarily call it a love affair, but it was definitely an affair that I loved. As I've said many times, I love myself a sex maniac. Or really, anyone who the majority of society would classify as having a "problematic sexuality." The problematic nature of his or her sexuality tends to be the variable, whether they're hypersexual to the point of self-destruction, or they're autistic and find sex awkward or annoying, or they're caught up in a sex scandal, or they're just kinda creepy in a way that would put most women off but for some reason makes me wet.

App Guy was all of the above. In moments when most of my other sexual partners would have told me *no*—"No, Karley, the cabdriver doesn't want to give you a back massage, go home, you're drunk"—App Guy always said *yes*, and then he'd egg me on even further. We'd get together a couple of times a month, usually in a hotel bar, and our goal generally became to see if we could pick up another girl on the fly. It always proved to be a fun challenge. We almost always failed, but the fun was mostly in seeing the reactions of the women, and the more repulsed they were by us, the funnier we found it. Who knew being turned down could be such a turn-on? App Guy was definitely sort of a weird sadist, and would often point out all the reasons that the girl at the other end of the bar was "unremarkable" and therefore sexually appealing. I suppose that sounds mean and potentially sexist (hence the "problematic" element), but App Guy's fault was more that he was an insecure idiot rather than a bad person, and he would never insult someone to their face. Admittedly, I'm not super proud of these moments—at *least* we were annoying, at most we were creepy, but we were always ultimately harmless. *But still.*

And then one day, App Guy ghosted. After five months of seeing each other. I was pretty hurt, honestly. Although, I'd sort of expected it would happen. Madeline had warned me about this. Part of the appeal of these sites is that you don't really owe anyone anything. The money acts as a barrier between you—no matter how much fun you have together or how many times you've fucked, the fact that you're on the payroll creates an undeniable, and often intentional, distance in the relationship. And when one person decides it's over, there's rarely a formal goodbye.

Over the next two years, SeekingArrangement changed my life pretty drastically. During that time I "dated" a handful of rich guys—five, to be exact. Some wonderful, some sad and lonely, some hot, some totally insane, all worth it. During this time I became un-poor, and the money I made allowed me the freedom to be a full-time writer. It felt like a huge weight had been lifted off my shoulders. I was financially comfortable for the first time in my life, which drastically reduced my levels of stress and anxiety. I felt more confident. And on a superficial level, the money meant that I could finally afford a good colorist so that my hair didn't look green in certain lights, and I was able to start wearing some (somewhat) nice clothes, which I'm pretty sure are both factors in why *Vogue* decided to hire me to write a column. Real talk.

I also genuinely liked the guys I met through the site. It made me feel stupid for having once bought into the all-too-common notion that all men who pay for sexual interactions must be creepy, ugly, exploitative, lonely trolls. There are many valid reasons why a man might hire a sex worker: because he is not looking for a relationship; because he wants the sex to stay casual; because he has a fetish that he feels comfortable opening up about only to someone he's paying; because he is turned on by the exchange of money; or, simply, because he's busy and getting an escort is just easier. Sometimes you're too lazy to go to a restaurant. Sometimes you're just in the mood for Seamless.

I'm not claiming that my experience as a sex worker

reflects everyone's. But I think it's valid to say that on SA I never felt exploited—or at least, not in a way that I couldn't handle. In fact, I felt far *less* exploited on SA than I did working for *Vice* or at other culture magazines, where my labor was clearly underappreciated and I was drastically underpaid. Don't get me wrong, there were definitely annoying things about SA. I went on some awful dates over the years, and I encountered a number of douchey guys through the site. But there are douches everywhere, and I've certainly gone on my share of awful Tinder dates. Sure, sometimes I'd be hungover in bed looking at memes, and the last thing on earth I'd want to do was go to the Upper West fucking Side and stroke some millionaire's ego and then have really performative sex—the *last thing on earth*. But in the end, I always felt like it was worth it, and ultimately more interesting than handing drunk people dumplings.

One time, while I interviewed the porn star Stoya, we were talking about how when you're a sex worker, people either victimize you or overpoliticize your work, but they often neglect to acknowledge the *practical* element of the job. Stoya told me, "People love to say 'We love that you're making a political statement with your body!' Or 'We love how money-motivated you are!' But I'm like…Um, I do porn because it sounded like fun, and like a great way to pay rent. And when it's not fun it's stuff I can deal with—aka how I would evaluate any other job." Solidarity.

the whorearchy

So why am I telling you all of this? And why now? As someone who regularly spills my guts on the internet as a profession, being on SA was notably a part of my life that I chose not to write about before this book.

One reason I've kept this a secret for so long is because, like most people, I have parents. Specifically, Catholic parents. And no matter how many times I say, "Mom and Dad, I promise, it was fun, I made good money, and I don't regret it," they will still not be thrilled to hear this news. I didn't write about it because I didn't want to submit myself to people's unwanted pity. I didn't want to feel like somehow, this information would taint my success as a writer—that people who thought I was successful enough to support myself from my writing alone would suddenly think less of me.

I ultimately decided to go there for a few reasons. For one, I had a feeling that my fear around this subject was somehow confirmation that it was exactly what I *should* be writing about. Also, I know that, when dealing with sexuality—or any other sensitive topic—it helps to hear the stories of people with experiences similar to our own, because it allows us to better understand our own experiences and our own bodies. It helps us to not feel so alone, basically. As I got deeper into the sugaring, and as I began to meet and interview other women in that world, I was shocked to learn how many women I *already knew* in New York, with ostensibly good jobs in creative industries, who were selling sex. Basically: New York rent prices + student debt + female sexual liberation = sex work. Maybe I should have been less surprised by this discovery, but it really shocked me—in a "Wow, that's badass" way, but also in a "It sucks that you can't make a decent living wage as a creative person in New York anymore" kind of way. In the seven years that I've lived in this city, most of the women I know who were able to sustain creative careers were those with rich parents and those who did sex work on the side, whether that be stripping, sugaring, domming, selling their underwear online, or letting a random man from craigslist smell their armpits (I know a girl who did that, FYI).

But despite the large number of smart, ambitious women doing sex work, there continues to be a negative, hackneyed stereotype around who sex workers are and how they got into their line of work. And it will be impossible to reinvent the image of the sex worker in the cultural consciousness until more sex workers feel safe to come out and tell their stories. As Camille Paglia said in her book *Vamps and Tramps* (1994): "Moralism and ignorance are responsible for the constant stereotyping of prostitutes by their lowest common denominator—the sick, strung-out addicts, crouched on city stoops, who turn tricks for drug money...The most successful prostitutes in history have been *invisible*. That invisibility was produced by their high intelligence, which gives them the power to perceive, and move freely but undetected within, the social frame...She is psychologist, actor, and dancer, a performance artist of hyper-developed sexual imagination." And today—if my personal foray into sugar-babying is any indication—she is the hipster sitting next to you at your bottomless mimosa brunch in the East Village. She is your future doctor and your future lawyer.

But being "invisible" as a sex worker is a privilege. And invisibility is something that sugar babies are afforded far more than women in other parts of the industry, particularly women who do street work, or who strip, who have no choice but to be on display. The fact that sugaring allows for some anonymity does not make it in any way "better" than other forms of sex work, nor does it mean that sugar babies are smarter, or more liberated, or more chic. But sugaring is the only part of this world that I have personal experience with.

However, after spending years interviewing and making friends with sex workers in various parts of the industry—from dommes to brothel workers to strippers and beyond—I've come to realize that when I first entered this world, I was a bit ignorant of my privilege. The reality check came during an interview I did with Tilly Lawless, a twenty-four-year-old queer sex worker and activist based in Sydney, Australia (where sex work is decriminalized). Tilly's a feral beauty, with a Cindy Crawford–esque mole and sandy-blond hair that hangs down to her waist. She's the sort of girl who can post photos on Instagram of herself riding naked on a horse through a field of flowers and somehow not look like a total poser idiot. It was Tilly who first explained the whorearchy to me. What's the whorearchy, you ask? Well, since Tilly can explain it far better than I can, here's a comprehensive breakdown, in her own words:

The whorearchy is the hierarchy that shouldn't—but does—exist in the sex industry, which makes some jobs within it more stigmatized than others, and some more acceptable. Basically it goes like this, starting from the bottom (in society's mind): street-based sex worker, brothel worker, rub-and-tug worker/erotic masseuse, escort, stripper, porn star, BDSM mistress, cam girl, phone sex worker, and finishing with sugar baby on the top. Sugar baby work is the most accepted as it's the closest to marriage in that it mimics monogamy and usually involves the exchange of material goods over cold hard cash (also, in a lot of places where sex work is illegal, sugar babying falls in a sort of legal grey space).

The whorearchy comes from both within and outside of the industry; non–sex workers will view certain workers as dirtier/more disposable/less worthy of respect than others, and sex workers themselves will often throw other workers under the bus, in order to distance themselves from them and make themselves seem more respectable. It's driven by assumptions and prejudice. While you will find people of all different races, backgrounds, and genders etc. in all different kinds of jobs within the sex industry, racist and classist assumptions feed into the whorearchy. For instance, a non-English-speaking, immigrant woman of color will be seen as "less valuable" than me (a white middle-class woman) and further down in the chain of things. Often, more marginalized people will be forced to work in lower rungs, for example trans women of color often won't be hired in brothels, and so have to do street-based sex work.

All sex workers are judged in this system. There is a (perceived) large gap between full-service (penetrative penis in vagina sex) and non-full-service sex work. For instance, when I crossed over from a rub-and-tug to working in a brothel, many of the girls said, "Yuck, that's disgusting." I have heard strippers describe themselves as "like a whore, but I keep my dignity." Escorts describe themselves as being "high class" in an attempt to market themselves, which suggests that other workers are low class, and feeds into the whorearchy and the idea that the rest of us are worthless. (I always say: "We are not deserving of rights and respect because we are high class, but because we are human.")

Sugar babies are some of the worst I have come across for playing into this. Because they are at the top of the whorearchy, they think they can shit on the rest of us and pretend their work is intrinsically different. "I'm not a prostitute/whore" is something I have heard time and time again from them, as if being a whore is a bad thing, or as if they don't also suck the cock of a man they aren't attracted to for gain.

People outside of the industry also judge you based on these misconceptions, too. A guy once said to me at a party, "Oh, but you're pretty. Don't call yourself a whore, you're not like those women I see on the street, don't class yourself with them," meaning it as a compliment.

The whorearchy is relevant because it has a lot to do with why I'm able to casually make jokes about being a whore. Because sugar babies fall into a legal gray area in America, we are able to engage in sex work without fear of arrest, and to talk about our jobs and our goals with less risk. Women working on the streets or in brothels might be equally liberated and educated as sugar babies, but they are less likely to tell their stories, because they face more consequences when they do. (Although, of course, there have been many radical and inspiring nonsugar sex workers over the years who told their stories in hopes that one day sex workers globally will have the same rights as any other person—for example, Xaviera Hollander, Carol Leigh, Jules Kim, Pye Jakobsson, Monica Jones, and Dr. Carol Queen, to name just a few.) And putting a face and a name to a sex worker helps us to be seen as individuals, rather than as statistics, or as the reductive stereotypes we see on TV (like a street-corner crackhead or a murdered body in a dumpster).

I was recently having a conversation over Skype with Norma Jean Almodovar, a prominent sex workers' activist and author of the book *Cop to Call Girl* (1994). Almodovar worked for the Los Angeles Police Department in the 1970s and early '80s before leaving to become a prostitute, because she felt like it was "more honest work" (amazing). When I asked Almodovar what type of woman does sex work, she responded flatly, "A practical woman." She told me, "The sugar baby phenomenon is a symptom of women being practical and saying, 'I don't want to put myself in huge debt for a good education.' These women are not being forced into sex work. They have simply realized that it's the quickest, fastest, easiest way to make a living."

But is it actually true, as the media often portrays it, that sites like SeekingArrangement have inspired millions of middle-class women who otherwise would never have considered sex work to start selling their bodies? Or has this been going on forever, and the internet has only made it more visible? "Street walkers have always been the smallest percentage of sex workers—less than fifteen percent—and yet they get the most attention," Almodovar told me. "Middle-class, educated women were always in the industry, advertising our services in magazines, working for high-class madams, working in safe brothels, fucking billionaires and famous actors, using our money to buy real estate and pay our tuitions—we just weren't visible. I know a lot of sex workers who were putting themselves through college before it was 'a thing.'"

And history supports this. For instance, a main argument in support of the birth control pill was that technology does not determine behavior—rather, technology *enables* behaviors that already exist. And studies have since validated this assertion: Unmarried women were having sex before the pill; it was just less out in the open. Similarly, people were having casual sex well before the dawn of Grindr and Tinder; dating apps have only made it more visible. And it's no secret that prostitution was a profession of many middle-class women before SeekingArrangement brought it aboveground and triggered a moral panic. "When it comes to sex work, there are recurring periods of moral crusades, which fade out and then come back into fashion," Almodovar told me. "People are endlessly offended by prostitution. What I find offensive is when people mind other people's business."

But people find great pleasure in involving themselves in the business of others, especially when it comes to women's bodies. Throughout history, women have repeatedly been told that we don't know what's best for us, and that other people should be left to make decisions about our health and our bodies. Just look at the conversations around birth control, abortion, and surrogacy for proof of this. The conversation around sex work is more of the same. In 2015, Amnesty International released a draft policy on the protection of the rights of sex workers, advocating for the full decriminalization of the sex industry. In reaction, a bunch of celebrities with "an opinion"—including Lena Dunham, Kate Winslet, Anne Hathaway, Meryl Streep, and Gloria Steinem—launched a campaign opposing the proposal, stating that "regardless of how a woman ends up in the sex trade, the abuse, sexual violence and pervasive injuries these women endure at the hands of their pimps and 'clients,' lead to lifelong physical and psychological harm—and, too often, death."

This statement is off base and factually incorrect. It follows a trend of inflammatory reporting on sex work that relies on inflated figures and false statistics that don't survive any serious analysis. Of course, no one should be forced into sex work, but consensual sex work and sex trafficking are *not the same thing* (despite being continuously conflated). To compare a woman being trafficked to an autonomous sex worker is the same as comparing a slave to an architect.

I was particularly bummed that Lena Dunham joined this crusade, considering that she touts a message of feminism and body positivity. Not to mention that she literally makes money from being naked on-screen, meaning that she has chosen to make her body a commodity. But it seems you can only do what you want with your body if it's something she deems to be okay. In reaction to the celebrity-led opposition, many sex workers have come forward online and essentially told these women to shut up and mind their own business. How patronizing of these (mostly privileged, white) celebrities to tell sex workers that they know more about what's right for their bodies? Weighing in on a situation that doesn't impact your life implies that the people who are actually impacted don't deserve to speak. They are silencing the voices of the sex worker who says, "I do not feel exploited." Not to mention that sex worker rights organizations, Human Rights Watch, and Amnesty International have all repeatedly pointed out that those who are *truly* interested in decreasing exploitation in the sex industry would be better off supporting the decriminalization of prostitution.

We should all have the right to make decisions about our own health, body, and sexuality, without fear, coercion, violence, or discrimination. And if a woman wants to finger a finance guy's butt in order to pay her bills, then she should pursue that dream, and the rest of us should move the fuck along. As porn star and writer Stoya told me, "There are many established academics out there today who truly believe that a woman having a public sexuality keeps us down—that it's this patriarchal plot. But porn isn't inherently more oppressive than anything else under capitalism. The problem with this branch of feminism is that, specifically when it comes to sex work, it neglects to consider capitalism. Like, what about the demonstrable wage disparity, and the fact that you can't have food and a roof over your head and medical care when you need it without money? And where the fuck is the money supposed to come from? Maybe [antiporn activist] Gail Dines skips to work at her office in the university, and would do her job even if she wasn't getting paid—but that's definitely not most people's lives."

Our own bodies can be tools for freedom. We can fuck for love or for fun or for money, but it should always be up to us to make that decision. And fucking for money can be more exciting than fucking for love, and fucking for fun can be more fun than fucking for money, and sometimes fucking for fun can turn out to be not so fun, because you expected it to be fun and then it was sort of boring. These are all valid experiences.

But sex work isn't just about money or freedom or feminism or politics—it's also about *sex*. Connecting money to sex is actually really hot, but it's something that nobody ever wants to talk about. When someone is willing to pay a thousand dollars to sleep with you, you don't need to be told that you're beautiful. You become a luxurious sex object, a living currency, and that can be a huge turn-on. It's impossible to have this experience with your partner because romantic relationships are too tied up in emotions. As a result, sex work provides a very unique sexual experience. People discount sex work as simply being a submission to money, or only being about power. But it's more than that: It's a sexual experience in itself, which is different than having sex for love or for fun.

We're a culture that finds perverse pleasure in shaming people who don't conform. People love to moralize, to point a finger and say, "You're worse than me." But shame usually has much more to do with the person doing the shaming than the person being shamed. What scares people the most about sex workers is the idea that they might actually *like* what they do. It forces people to admit that they don't deplore sex work only because they feel sorry for its apparent victims, but because maybe, just maybe, sex workers are getting away with something that they're not.

from slut to bi
chapter 5

gay propaganda

I *don't identify as bisexual.* I just identify as a slut, which is basically the same thing anyway, right? My mother thinks so.

Until I met Alice, I never expected that I would be in a serious relationship with a woman. That's not because I didn't try. I mean, I'm a sex blogger—it would clearly be on brand for me to have a gay moment. Instant feminist street cred, ya know? However, while I've always maintained many strong female friendships, and have found myself repeatedly in awe of women in a friend-crush sort of way, up until my midtwenties my romantic experiences with women never seemed to progress further than just being a fleeting "sex thing." I felt doomed for straightness. Sure, I was a straight girl who sometimes casually ended up with a vagina in my mouth, but a straight girl just the same.

There were a few girls over the years who gave me butterflies. Most notably JD Samson, the gender-bending drummer from Le Tigre. JD's oversize tuxedos and sort-of-mustache had my vagina tingling in blissful confusion for most of my early twenties. Then there was my friend Jill, the delicate, heroin-chic model with a boyish figure and a cliché beat-up biker jacket whose bed I ended up in a few times during that same period. She was the first girl I ever slept with one-on-one (i.e., not in an MDMA-induced chaotic group sex situation). But with Jill, I was always unsure of whether I actually wanted to be *with* her, or I just wanted to *be* her—like, in a creepy, wear-your-skin type of way.

It was during my early squat years, when I was about nineteen, that I became friends with a group of women who I'm still close with to this day. They were a bit older than me, in their mid- to late twenties, and were all either gay or sexually fluid. I remember being intrigued and kind of envious of their relationships—they appeared to have intense levels of intimacy and understanding with their female partners. They were like regular girlfriends—they talked about periods and calories, and shared clothes and vaginal antifungal creams—but they one-upped it by adding sex (and sex that was apparently multiorgasmic, which at the time was a foreign concept to me). À la Carrie Bradshaw, I couldn't help but wonder…is lesbianism the ultimate life hack?

"Being with women is *the best*," Lolo told me. Lolo was the French, bisexual, astrology-obsessed member of our group, and at twenty-five she was in her first serious gay relationship. "With girls you can have sex for *hours and hours*, because you're not at the mercy of the guy's boner," she swooned. I told her that sounded nice, but also exhausting and painful. "Plus," she added, "you can make out forever without getting a rash, because girls don't have beards." That last part really resonated with me, because I happen to be quite a rashy person.

Something I loved about hanging with the lesbian mafia was the novelty of being with a group of women who didn't devote a huge amount of time to talking about men. It was basically like that episode of *Sex and the City* when Charlotte becomes enamored with a group of power lesbians, and after realizing that they've seemingly found a loophole to male emotional ineptitude, she becomes desperate to be in their club. Except instead of a group of ubersuccessful art-world lesbians with vacation homes in the Hamptons, my lesbians were aspiring DJs chugging cheap vodka from flasks in south London squat raves. But I loved them just the same. Of course, I know the idea of "gay propaganda" is controversial. Though to be honest, these girls were a strong advertisement for team lez.

But it wasn't until years later, just after my twenty-seventh birthday, that I met Alice. Our story begins as any great hipster romance should: at the *Vice* New York office. At the time, I was making a satirical sex-ed video series for the company, and Alice was called in to help with postproduction. I'd been sitting in a tiny editing cubicle chugging kombucha for twelve straight hours (as one does in a hipster sweatshop) and was on the verge of a web series–induced mental breakdown when in walked Alice: a tall, dimpled genderqueer Spanish cutie. She held up a bottle of vodka with her scrawny arm and smiled a big, toothy smile. I was sold.

Has it ever happened to you that, upon meeting a complete stranger, you instantly have the overwhelming urge to rest your head on their stomach and stay that way forever? It's not even necessarily a sexual urge. The feeling is more abstract—more innocent, somehow. Well, that's how I felt when I saw her. Like, it wasn't *just* that I wanted to fuck her; I also wanted to stick my head under her faded T-shirt and fall asleep. About twenty minutes later, after the initial dizziness began to fade, I realized this was the first time I'd felt such crazy butterflies for a woman.

After that first night, I played the normal dating game—I stalked her online, intensely scrutinized the social media of everyone she'd ever dated, and then forced our one mutual friend to have a party at her apartment where we could "accidentally" run into each other again. Unbeknownst to me, this mutual friend immediately texted Alice saying, "By the way, Karley forced me to have this party as an excuse to hang out with you." Weak move. Clearly, I showed up to the party pretending to be all aloof and casual, which made me look like a total idiot, but a cute idiot, apparently, because Alice and I ended up drunkenly banging in the hallway of the apartment building that very evening. Later that night, back at her apartment, we took a shower and I washed her hair, a uniquely sweet moment in spite of having known each other only briefly. And then I masturbated while she choked me.

After that, we became instantly and almost parasitically

inseparable. And just like in my youthful lesbian fantasies, I came *every time* we fucked. Sometimes twice. This was a completely new—*bizarre*, even—experience for me after years of dating Max, whose idea of making me come was to doze off while laying his limp hand over my boob while I used my vibrator. Romantic. But Alice would ask me what felt good, and then she would just *do* exactly what I liked—how novel! And Lolo was right: You *can* have marathon sex sessions for hours, because you're not a slave to the boner. It was a lesbian miracle. As a lesbian friend of mine said in response to the controversially long girl-on-girl sex scenes in *Blue Is the Warmest Color*: "Straight couples have sex for like five minutes, but lesbians have sex for like five hours, so if you look at the ratio, it makes sense that a lesbian sex scene in movie time would be twenty minutes long."

However, despite everything being physically great, for the first few months we were together, I found it hard to fully "lose myself" during sex. Often, during particularly sweet or passionate moments, I'd suddenly become extremely aware of myself, almost as if I were looking down at us from above like a pervy guardian angel. And then I'd think: "Wait, *weird*...I'm, like, gay now randomly?" Clearly, this would jolt me out of the moment. It felt like such a stupid thought to be having, but I couldn't seem to stop it from repeatedly inserting itself into my brain. Like, you know how when you go to a party wearing an outfit that's different from what you'd normally wear, and even though you like the outfit, you don't feel super comfortable in it yet, and so instead of being your cool, natural self, you just keep anxiously checking yourself out in the mirror? Well, that's what being in your first gay relationship is like, in a nutshell.

These moments of hyper-self-awareness didn't just occur during sex. Often, when we rode the subway together, Alice would put her hand on my knee and suddenly I'd think, *Everyone on this train thinks I'm a lesbian.* I wasn't noting it because it made me feel bad or self-conscious; I was just registering that it was *different.* We all naturally become accustomed to the role we play in society and the way the outside world perceives us. Like, I'm a busty blonde who's usually wearing a push-up bra and a pink miniskirt—I push femininity to the point of parody. When I'm out in the world, subconsciously or not, everyone perceives me as a straight girl with a low IQ. I'd grown comfortable with that. It's what I knew. We all make assumptions about people based on the way they look all the time, and that's totally normal and intuitive. (For instance, if you're a guy with a ponytail, tribal tattoos, and low-rise jeans, I know that you've been to a sex party in the past month, and that you probably have massage oil in your man-bag at this very moment.) However, no matter what you look like, when you're a woman holding hands with another woman, in the eyes of everyone else, you're gay. *Maybe* bi, but probably gay, because bisexuality is essentially invisible in everyday life. Like, what does a bi person look like? It's pretty much impossible to identify someone as bisexual, unless they're literally walking down the street with a man on one arm and a woman on the other, making out with both (life goals).

Over time, this self-awareness faded as I became more comfortable in my relationship. But the most significant adjustment wasn't getting used to being feministly fisted, or to the new way that people stared at me on the L train. It was about reassessing *myself* and what was important to me. It wasn't just that I suddenly felt compelled to watch YouTube videos with titles like "The Gay Rights Movement Explained in 5 Minutes." Yes, that absolutely happened, but it was bigger than that. After meeting Alice, I felt like I was being shown new possibilities for what my life could look like. It's not like I was ever one of those creeps who treats life as a search for a husband. But at the risk of sounding conventional, since I was young, the vague image I had created of my future always involved a tweedy, intellectual husband, a *Rosemary's Baby*–esque Manhattan apartment, and a couple of unusually gifted children. It never involved sharing tampons and yeast infection cream, or being deeply understood by my partner in ways I never thought possible (a terrifying prospect, really). But my feelings for my girlfriend were changing my idea of what forever looked like. I was like, *Fuck, could this be the person who I want to make love and kale salad with* forever? And this sudden shift left me staring at my reflection in my iPhone, having Zoolander-esque "Who am I?" moments.

bisexual demons

It probably won't surprise you to hear that when I told my Catholic mother that I was in a serious relationship with a gender-nonbinary lesbian Jew, she basically wanted to nail herself to a cross. At first, she was mad that I had lied to her by omission, having kept the relationship a secret from her for more than a year. This, admittedly, wasn't so cool on my part. But cut me some slack—clearly I had avoided telling my parents about Alice because I knew it wasn't going to go over well. However, phase two of my mother's meltdown really surprised me. What she said was "So you're telling me that your whole life has been a lie? You've been a lesbian *all these years* and you never told me? I feel like I don't even know you!" This was followed by waterworks, while I tried to keep a straight face (like as in literally trying to appear heterosexual).

I spent the following hours—and weeks, and months—trying to explain the reality of my situation to my her: "Mom," I'd say, "my life hasn't been a lie. I just randomly fell in love with a woman. It's very Millennial." She didn't buy it. In fact, it made the situation even worse. In her mind, if I was gay (as she insisted I must be) it would be tragic, but at least she understood what being gay meant. She knew gay people. She thought Anderson Cooper was hot. A lesbian daughter, in theory, could give her grandchildren. But my being bi was horrifying, because if the unspeakable myth known as bisexuality actually existed, it meant that not only did I fuck women, but that I was essentially a sex-crazed zombie willing to fuck *anything and everyone*. Being gay was deviant, but being bisexual was just greedy, like the all-you-can-eat strip-mall Chinese buffet version of sexual orientation.

This perception of bisexuality is not uncommon. For the most part, people assume either that bisexuality doesn't exist, or that bi people are evil sluts, basically. And these ideas are heavily reflected in popular culture. When I was growing up, bi people were practically invisible in the mainstream. And when they were represented, they were usually killing someone. Literally. Like, have you ever noticed that bisexual people in movies are almost always sex-crazed demonic murderers? Just to throw out a few examples: There's the classic thriller *Basic Instinct*, where Sharon Stone plays a depraved, murderous bisexual; or *Jennifer's Body*, where Megan Fox engages in a sex ritual that transforms her into a bisexual homicidal demon; or *House of Cards*, in which the protagonist Frank Underwood is a manipulative, sexually fluid politician who casually kills anyone who gets in the way of his rise to power. And these are just the most obvious examples.

In an article for *Slutever*, writer Kristen Cochrane shed light on the tired stereotypes and tropes that are projected onto bisexuals. Her essay explored how negative representations of bi people reinforce hegemonic definitions of good and evil—good often being equated with normativity and dominant values, and evil often being equated with transgression. And bisexuality is often presented as the ultimate threat to normative order and humanity's very existence. To quote Cochrane:

> Bisexuals are often characterized as the villain. A quick Google search led me to find a TV Tropes page that discussed the recurrence of the "Depraved Bisexual" in moving-image media. It's a simultaneously funny yet tragic encyclopedic web page which outlines how the "Depraved Bisexual" is different from the "Psycho Lesbian" trope. Instead of being an angry, crazy lesbian, the "Depraved Bisexual" is always down for sex, and will take whatever they can, whenever they can. These assumptions lead to many people feeling entitled to ask the "Depraved Bisexual" about their sex life (e.g. if you are female, how you have sex with other women, "Does this mean you will have a threesome with me and my girlfriend?" asks the straight guy, usually, etc.)...It is evidentiary of the objectification of queer people.

In 2016, GLAAD's annual "Where We Are on TV Report," analyzing the state of LGBTQ characters on scripted television, showed that bi characters are on the rise, making up roughly 30 percent of recurring LGBT television personalities. Clearly, this sounds like progress. However, while gay and lesbian TV characters are increasingly being portrayed in a way that doesn't make their sexuality a primary and morally reprehensible element of their character, bi characters are still often represented as

two-dimensional clichés. There are four main tropes surrounding bisexuality, as identified by GLAAD: (1) characters who are depicted as untrustworthy, prone to infi-
delity, and/or lacking a sense of morality; (2) characters
who use sex as a means of manipulation or who lack the
ability to form genuine relationships; (3) associations
with self-destructive behavior; (4) treating a character's
attraction to more than one gender as a temporary plot
device that is rarely addressed again.

The truth is, I've always been hesitant to identify as bisexual, and not *just* because of the demonic murderer association. For one, the word "bisexual" just sounds a bit old-
school at this point. A lot of people that are in theory
bisexual—in the sense that they are attracted to both men
and women—are *also* attracted to people in other gender
categories, like trans women, trans men, and any number of
the other roughly nine thousand confusing Facebook gender
options, like snake gender or whatever the Gen Zs are into.

For the most part, people either think bisexuality is
"just a phase"—like an "I did a lot of 'experimenting'
[read: drugs] in college" type of thing—or they assume
bisexuality is simply a stepping stone on the way to a gay
identity. Or, worse, they think identifying as bi just means
you're in gay denial. That last one is especially true for
men. Take my friend Joseph, for instance. He's a twenty-
six-year-old artist who predominantly sleeps with guys.
However, like me, he occasionally finds himself face-to-
face with a pussy. Nothing to make a fuss about. However,
when asked about his sexual identity, he always just says

he's gay, "because it's *easier*." He said that in the past, when he's identified as bi, people just assumed he was too embarrassed to wear a badge of gayness. So, to avoid presenting an image of shame, he just sticks with gay. I get where he's coming from, but it's still a bummer.

Some people assume that if you identify as bi, you have to be simultaneously involved with both genders to be truly satisfied. Basically, your life is a never-ending threesome, or else you're bored. This leads to the erroneous belief that bisexual people must be either nonmonogamous or promiscuous (which is actually true in my case, so I'm not a great example, whoops). Also, if you're a bi woman, sometimes a guy will assume that you're just hooking up with another woman as a tactic to get his dick hard. Because we all know that female sexuality really only exists as an aphrodisiac for men.

After I started eating pussy on a regular basis, I felt like I needed to find a new way to identify my sexuality now that straight was no longer cutting it, and so began my quest for the perfect trademark. For a second I considered "straight but with a girlfriend," which Alice quickly vetoed. Then came the awkward explanation "I just have a very egalitarian vagina." Also not popular. After that I tried out "down for whatever" for a while. I liked how casually confident it sounded, like something you'd say with a shrug while sipping a martini. However, people at parties kept misinterpreting this as me wanting to immediately blow them in the bathroom, so I unfortunately had to extinguish that as well.

On some days my search for an identifier seemed irrelevant. *Fuck it*, I'd think. *I'm a liberated sexual butterfly—who cares what word I use?* But on other days I felt like a sexual orphan, not totally at home in the gay or straight communities. Essentially, homeless.

Words are power. Having the right language can help us to carve out our place in the world, whether that label be doctor, mother, slut, athlete, groupie…whatever. Labels can build communities and empower through solidarity. But other times, they can limit us. Like, just because you identify as gay, that means that you're never, *ever* allowed to sleep with someone of the opposite sex? Even if you're high on ecstasy? *Come on.* If cool, smart, nice, hot people come in all shapes, sizes, ages, races, and genders, then why should we assign ourselves some dumb label that will only inhibit us from tasting the rainbow?

And then it came to me one day, while I was attempting to do Pilates. I was bending over to touch my toes, and I thought, *Gosh, I'm so flexible.* Like a classic epiphany, it hit me.

That was a lie. But "flexible" *is* a word I've only recently adopted, and it's the first word that instantly felt right in association with my sexuality. *Flexible*—someone whose sexuality can bend and change, even accommodate; a state so elastic that it's impossible to classify. Sure, in a sense, "flexible" is still a label, but it's also kind of not, somehow. It's a nonlabel label? It describes an identity without subscribing to an identity. It's like the sex equivalent of being agnostic. It's the ultimate noncommitment (and you know I'm a commitmentphobe).

In the past, there've been a variety of other labels that people have adopted in order to separate themselves from the norm and to assert that sexuality exists on a spectrum. For instance: omnisexual, pansexual, polysexual, queer, sexually fluid, gay-for-pay, et cetera. I know many people who identify as queer, and who get a lot out of feeling like part of that community. However, all these identifiers are a bit too heavy-handed for me, personally. They don't stand *purely* for the freedom of desire; rather, they represent lifestyles that come with a prepackaged set of ideas. And I'm wary of that baggage. I hate the idea that if I tell someone I'm queer, they already have all these predetermined ideas about me—what music I like, what bars I hang out in, that I go to poetry readings at feminist bookstores and braid my armpit hair and am furiously vegan…or whatever.

In a *Big Think* interview about religion, the famous astrophysicist Neil deGrasse Tyson said, "I don't associate with movements—I think for myself. The moment someone attaches you to a philosophy or a movement, they then assign all the baggage and the rest of the philosophy that goes with it to you. And when you want to have a conversation, they will assert that they already know everything important there is to know about you because of that association."

What I'm getting at with this longwinded rant is, it feels good to remove my sexuality from the burden of any type of dogma. I'm not exaggerating when I say that I flip my Tinder settings back and forth from men to women depending on how I'm feeling that day. Sometimes it genuinely feels like my sexuality changes with the fucking wind.

sexual yoga

In 2018, we pat ourselves on the back for being sexually progressive, gender-defiant, morally superior posteverything children of wokery. However, new studies show that sexual fluidity existed long before the dawn of the feminist blogosphere. The idea that not everyone is either exclusively straight or exclusively gay, or consistently somewhere in the middle, isn't a new one. The revolutionary sex researcher Alfred Kinsey developed the Kinsey scale way back in 1948, which placed sexuality on a continuum of 0 to 6: "exclusively heterosexual" to "exclusively homosexual." Since then, there've been various liberal pockets of society in which people have accepted ideas about sexual fluidity, from the free-love hippies in the 1960s to the rise of queer culture in San Francisco in the '90s. However, to our credit, only in recent years have we begun to accept sexual flexibility in a broader, more mainstream social sense. In other words, sexual fluidity is no longer a fringe idea—it's now used by Calvin Klein to sell underwear. When we can capitalize on our bisexuality, we know we've truly made progress.

Today, there's a growing body of social science research indicating that a substantial number of people experience fluidity in their sexual and romantic attractions. Reliable data from several recent studies found that 6 to 9 percent of American men and 10 to 14 percent of American women describe themselves as not completely heterosexual—they wouldn't necessarily identify as bisexual, but they fall somewhere in the gray area. (For reference, 1 to 2 percent of the male population is gay, and 1 percent or less of the female population is lesbian.) Yes, the vast majority of the world is still straight—even though it really doesn't seem that way if you live in New York—but the verdict at the core of much of this new data is clear: Sexual variability is a natural part of being human.

The Gen Zs are the most liquid of all. They make even Millennials look square. Of course, it's difficult to get exact statistics when it comes to sexual identity and behavior, but based on my own personal, not-at-all scientific analysis of the situation, I'm pretty sure that everyone below the age of twenty-six identifies as a radical queer nongendered entity. Sounds exhausting, if you ask me. Take my little brother, for example. He's a twenty-six-year-old Vassar grad, and whenever I hang out with him and all his liberal-arts-school deep-Brooklyn vegan performance-art friends, I feel so fucking old and out of touch. Like, my bro is currently in a throuple with two people whose preferred gender pronouns are "they." I mean, you do you (or they do them, I guess?) but that just sounds super complicated to me. It's funny how every generation goes through the same transition—essentially from being like "Parents just don't understand!" to "Kids these days are fucking nuts."

The point is, never before have we had so many options—about who we are, how we live, who we date, how we fuck, and the structure of our relationships. And even if I love making fun of the Gen Zs and their creepily self-serious green-haired identity politics, I do feel excited to live in a time when people are afforded so much personal freedom. Like, twenty years ago, if you were a gay dude, you by default wore lip gloss, obsessed over Dior, and then grew up to become the weird uncle who never gets married and spends a suspect amount of time with his roommate. If you were a gay woman, you were obligated to wear frumpy blazers and become a gym teacher. It was a simpler time. But today, you can be gay and do whatever you want. You can be a gay athlete. You can be a gay spouse. You can be a gay Kristen Stewart. God, the tyranny of choice!

Increased cultural visibility has been integral to this shift. In the last decade, American TV shows and movies have begun to showcase more complex LGBTQ characters than ever before—and even bisexual representation is starting to be less demonic. Popular shows like *Revenge*, *Transparent*, and *Broad City* all feature bi characters who are distinctly not murderers. And I've seen firsthand how influential this type of representation can be. About a year into my relationship with Alice, my mom started watching *Orange Is the New Black*. If you've never seen it, the main character is a bisexual woman named Piper. Sure, she's a convicted drug smuggler, but she's ultimately a good and likable person. Literally within days of watching the show, my mom called me saying, "*Oooh*, I get it now—you're like Piper!" It didn't matter how much I'd personally explained my sexuality to her—she needed to see it on TV for it to be truly real. And you could see that as depressing, but I chose to be more optimistic than that. And while I can't say my mother ever fully got on board with my gay relationship, over time I could tell that watching and loving shows like *OITNB* and *Transparent* made her far more curious and understanding of sexual switch-hitters. Visibility is power, because we cannot be what we cannot see.

The recent increase in visibility of people who are "in the middle"—whether it's packs of bisexual supermodels, or college campuses full of "theys"—has allowed space for more people to come out and explore these in-between identities for themselves. But this has been a process. Basically, it took gay and trans identities becoming more accepted in order for sexually flexible and genderqueer people to be able to come out, too. It's only when the *extremes* become accepted that people feel free to meander through the gray area.

Of course, many people are born gay, and their same-sex attraction is nonnegotiable. I don't believe that a gay person can just choose to be straight, in some insane Mike Pence "ex-gay therapy" sort of way. But I also think that there are a lot of people out there like me—people who were taught as kids that you're either gay or straight, and who felt comfortable enough in one of those categories to never really question it. We didn't know what else was on the menu. Because I'm attracted to plenty of men, if I had been born thirty or maybe even ten years earlier, I most likely would have lived a straight life, and perhaps not thought about all the lesbian orgasms I was potentially missing. But because I live in a morally bankrupt cosmopolitan liberal bubble of sluttiness, I was like, "Eh, why not give gay a try?"

I could see this in Alice when we were together, too. When we met she identified as a woman—at least, on most days—but her clothing, hair, and mannerisms all were what would classically be described as "teenage stoner bro." Whenever we would walk into a restaurant and the hostess would say something along the lines of "Good evening, ladies," I'd notice her flinch. The reality was, she didn't like being seen as a girl. She would lament over having to use the women's restroom, in part because she looked like a boy and walking into the ladies' room usually resulted in some woman telling her she was in the wrong bathroom. However, as time went on, and as transgender culture became the only thing anyone ever wanted to talk about, she became more comfortable with expressing herself as being in the gender gray zone. "In between" suddenly felt like a valid place to hang out.

In the wake of this new openness to flexibility, it's natural to ask yourself: Is my life *better* today because I have the opportunity for sexual exploration? Obviously freedom and self-exploration are good things, but if you don't know what you're missing, how can you miss it? Basically, would my quality of life really have been worse without the freedom to be fucked with a strap-on? I guess you could argue that ignorance is bliss. But looking back on how much I learned and gained in my queer relationship, I can't imagine not having had that opportunity. My time with Alice was undoubtedly the most adult, loving, supportive, and sexually fulfilling partnership that I'd ever been in. It changed me deeply—as all good relationships should. Alice was a great communicator, and she taught me that if something between us was bothering me, I should just talk to her about it, rather than act like a passive-aggressive cunt for a week and then randomly fuck someone I met on the subway out of spite (aka my strategy in all my previous relationships). She taught me that I was multiorgasmic, that being fisted is overrated, and that it's possible to be in a relationship where you know, without question, that your partner has your back. And most importantly, being with her taught me that a relationship can be a partnership between two equals. As Rebecca Solnit wrote in her book *Men Explain Things to Me*, "A marriage between two people of the same gender is inherently egalitarian—one partner may happen to have more power in any number of ways, but for the most part it's a relationship between people who have equal standing and so are free to define their roles themselves. Gay men and lesbians have already opened up the question of what qualities and roles are male and female in ways that can be liberating for straight people."

At the core of the slut lifestyle is the ability to be sexually curious and activated without shame. And as we grow more tolerant, and as we continue to expand the sexual menu, the slut mode of operation is just more attainable. A world without sexual borders is less about transgressing into taboo—as many conservatives and sex-negative people have long predicted—and more about emotional honesty. Soon, people will no longer be burdened to "come out." People won't be presumed murderers simply for being 40 percent gay (and 60 percent gay when drunk). We will just be people, wandering the earth, looking for hot people to fuck. And what could be more authentic than that?

wait...what is sex, even?
(and is that flexible too?)
chapter 6

subchapter: opening my mind and legs

*A*nyone who's read Miranda July's fiction knows *that it's* never a good sign when you relate to her characters. They tend to be lonely, insecure, and plagued by a twee sexual awkwardness, like hipsters having sex at a Belle and Sebastian concert in a Wes Anderson movie. No matter how much you love her writing, when you see yourself in her creations, it's always paired with an existential cringe.

When I first read July's book of short stories, *No One Belongs Here More Than You*, in my early twenties, it all felt a little too real. One part of the story "Mon Plaisir," in particular, really got to me. It begins with a couple lying in bed, talking about their sex life. "You still like it *our way*, don't you?" the woman asks. You soon find out what she means by that. "We did it in our way," July writes. "Carl nursed and I jacked him off. Then I turned away and touched myself while Carl patted the back of my head. I came."

I went over and over those four sentences in my head. *Does that count as sex?* I wondered. Based on what I'd learned growing up, there seemed to be a limited number of ways that two people could interact that could be qualified as "sex," and this didn't fit the bill. Surely that was just hooking up, or second base, or tragedy…but not *S-E-X*.

The reason I was so preoccupied with this story was that it reminded me of a period of my life that was defined by a particular sexual insecurity—specifically, an insecurity about whether I was even having sex at all. You might have called it a crisis of fucking. Or a fucking crisis. Or just fucking awkward.

I was eighteen when I met Sam, in a park near campus, soon after I arrived in London for university. One evening, while stumbling back to my dorm, I ran into some people drinking wine on the grass who looked attractive enough to muster up some drunken energy for. We were all freshmen, navigating that clumsy-yet-exciting phase of college where you feel like you're finally an adult in charge of a newfound sexual agency, when in reality you're just having blacked-out sex with DJs and setting your house on fire when trying to boil spaghetti. (This is actually the *only* phase of college I ever had to navigate—remember, I dropped out after one semester, because I'm lazy and/or a genius.) I walked over to the group, and by chance I sat down next to Sam, a smiley nineteen-year-old with a big mop of tangled dyed-black hair, wearing a tattered vintage suit that he'd mended with safety pins and electrical tape á la a homeless person. His ripped clothing hung limply off his lanky body, and he had these elegant collarbones that jutted out beneath his pink freckled skin.

His nails were painted sparkly black, and he was absently strumming "Wonderwall" on an acoustic guitar. As we talked, it wasn't so much that there were butterflies in my stomach as huge bats. (Today, I think acoustic guitars need a trigger warning, but back then they were basically porn. Remember, this was when I made style-inspiration mood boards that heavily featured Christina Aguilera.)

The first thing I noticed about Sam—aside from the fact that he looked like the personification of "backpacking around Europe"—was his voice: deep and powerful, but also soft, with a feminine quality. I was mesmerized. (Being a new transplant, I was still in the phase where I thought British people sounded exotic, rather than like frogs pretending to be fancy.) He told me about his band, which he'd started when he was sixteen, and who were about to release their first record. Everything about Sam seemed intimidatingly cool and foreign to me. He told me that he'd spent half of his childhood living in a castle north of London, and the other half in Sweden, but that his family usually summered in Morocco, which is where he learned to play the tbilat drums. I told him that I grew up in the same town as Snooki, and that my family vacationed at the Jersey Shore, which was where I'd developed my taste for fried shrimp. When he asked me what I was passionate about, I replied enthusiastically, "Well, I'm really good at soccer," to which he responded, "What's soccer?" We had a lot in common.

It wasn't until an hour later, when Sam got up to leave, that I noticed he walked with crutches—specifically, metal crutches that had been sloppily decorated with blue sparkles and an array of shiny stickers. I assumed he'd broken his leg or something, and didn't mention it. We exchanged numbers and made vague plans to meet up again. But as soon as he left I got that cheesy heart-sinking feeling that people write bad poems about, and I ended up chasing him down the street. "Sorry," I said, out of breath. "I just missed you." We made out. It felt very low-budget rom-com. I invited him back to my place, but he made an excuse about being tired and then crutched off into the night, leaving me horny and alone, clutching a bottle of cheap cider. I was slightly appalled, honestly. I've always felt that, as a general rule, if someone tries to have sex with you, you should have sex with them back—it's only polite.

On our second date, after pounding vodka Red Bulls at the university bar and then aggressively dry-humping back at his house, Sam told me that he had permanently damaged his spine in a childhood accident, after which he was never able to walk without the assistance of medical crutches and leg braces that started at his feet and came up over his knees, Forrest Gump–style. And then he dropped that he was a virgin. I think I was more thrown off by the virginity than the disability, honestly.

My first question was: "Can you have sex?" That probably sounds insensitive, but it made sense in context—I mean, I was literally straddling him in a bedazzled push-up bra. He laughed and said that yes, he could have sex, but he just hadn't…yet. He told me he wanted to "take things slow" because he "really liked me," saying that sex would be more meaningful if we waited until we felt close to one another. I pretended to agree, but inside, my brain was quietly short-circuiting. Getting to know someone *before* you fuck? It seemed a bizarre concept. Surely people had sex to assess if they *wanted* to get to know someone, not the other way around. It's just the Millennial way.

Sam and I dated for basically infinity before we slept together. I was a virgin to delayed gratification, but Sam refused to fuck me, and of course it made me fall in love with him. Anytime he gave me permission to be around him, I would drop everything to be by his side. I started skipping classes so that I could sit on the sidelines and watch his band practice, like a budget Yoko-in-training. I'd spend money I didn't have on train tickets to middle-of-nowhere Wales to surprise him at his gigs. I couldn't remember a time when I had been so tragically unaloof. I kept thinking, *Is this the trick my mom taught me when I was thirteen, which I promptly ignored?* Ya know: If you want someone to like you, don't sleep with them right away? Apparently nothing gets me wet like rejection.

For months we would kiss and grope, but that's as far as it got. On multiple occasions, while making out, I tried to sneakily unbutton Sam's pants without him noticing, which always resulted in him annoyedly swatting my hand away. More than once I thought to myself, *Wait…am I a rapist?* We would often sleep in the same bed, but Sam would keep all his clothes on—like, no lie, even his shoes. Each night we'd get under the covers and he would turn his back to me, and I'd just lie there and wait for his breathing to change, so that I knew he was asleep, and then I'd ever-so-quietly stick my hands down my tights and make myself come to the sound of his light snoring. I'm sure all these anecdotes are making me sound super sane.

I understand now, looking back on it all, that a big reason Sam wanted to wait was because he wasn't confident in his body. But of course, when you're an insecure teenager, everything is about *me*—what's wrong with *me*, and woe is *me*, and *my* feelings are hurt, and *I'm* desperate for dick, et cetera. I was needy and wore my heart on my sleeve—a dangerous combination—and since we weren't having sex, I constantly prodded Sam for other forms of validation. I cringe thinking about this now, but in those first few months of dating I actually *asked him* to write a song about me. That's straight-up psych ward–level behavior. Surely that tops the list of things you should never ask someone you've just started dating, even worse than "Where is this going?" However, instead of immediately deleting my number, he actually wrote me the song. How unironically romantic? I took this as a sign that he must like me for *me*, because he clearly wasn't just tolerating my personality in exchange for all the sex we weren't having.

I can rationally understand why Sam might have been insecure about being naked with me, but I loved the way he looked. I loved that he was thin but strong. Walking around on crutches for years had made his arms and chest quite muscular, but in an athletic, statue-of-David way, rather than a creepy whey-protein way. I liked that his body was unique. He was beautiful, but he didn't look like anyone else—both in terms of his body, and the fact that he dressed like Edward Scissorhands at the Warped Tour. I think one of his main concerns was that he wouldn't be able to fuck me "adequately"—or, at least, how other guys in the past had fucked me. If only he knew how low the bar was.

As we became closer, I tried to talk to him about all of this—about how he didn't have to be nervous around me, and I wasn't going to judge him, and I thought he was so hot, and blah blah blah please get your dick out. And it was sort of working. But then I made the mistake of telling about my aforementioned childhood obsession with Colin, the freckle-faced, wheelchair-bound character from *The Secret Garden*. "I used to masturbate to that scene of him angrily wheeling around the garden," I told Sam enthusiastically. In my blond head, this seemed like a funny anecdote to tell him in the midst of our serious discussion about body confidence and the future of our sex life—like a "See, I'm into disabled guys, don't worry," *wink wink* type of thing. He was not pleased.

The issue, which I stupidly did not realize would be an issue, was that he started to think I was fetishizing him. He told me that he wanted me to be into him *despite* his disability, not because of it—a sentiment he often repeated throughout the course of our relationship. In my defense, the whole *Secret Garden* thing was just a coincidence. Before meeting Sam, I was never "into disabled guys" (or *not* into them). I was just trying to lighten the mood with an offensive anecdote, okay? Of course, I did love Sam "for him," and I by no means wanted to fuck him out of pity. Or because of some power thing where I got off on him being "less able" than me. Or because the metal on his legs looked vaguely bondage. Or, for the record, because he made me wait and I just loved the chase (our four years together is surely proof of that). Let's be real, I was eighteen—I mainly wanted to fuck him because he was in a band.

Eventually, after three months of dry-humping and so much making out that I had a perma-rash on my chin, little by little we began to "fool around." And those first sexual interactions both enlightened and confused the fuck out of my teenage mind. Because of the ability of Sam's body, we couldn't have sex in a lot of the "normal" positions. Me on top was cool, but at this stage penetrative sex wasn't even remotely on the menu. At the beginning, it usually went down like this: We'd get into bed, I'd strip naked, and then he would just sort of inspect my body while jerking off, still wearing most of his clothes, usually to the soundtrack of Arcade Fire. At first it was more innocent, like he'd give me a gentle massage, lightly touching the outside (only the outside!) of my body, and then we'd both masturbate. Then it slowly evolved into a doctor-patient role play where he'd literally give me an exam, checking me for cancer and crabs and spending an unprofessional amount of time just staring blankly at my vagina (to be fair, it was the first one he'd ever seen not on a porn star, but to this day I've never had someone do such a thorough inspection, medical or not). Eventually the exam began including him sticking his fingers inside me. I think it was somewhere around month four that I was finally given permission to take off his pants.

While all of this was going on, I was constantly analyzing these experiences with my roommate, a red-haired girl with more than one Bob Marley poster in her bedroom. "Are we having sex? Have Sam and I had sex?!" I'd ask her, panicked. It's funny: Before then, there were multiple times when I had fucked a guy in a car for like forty seconds while completely wasted, I could barely feel anything (let alone come), there was no emotional connection, I could only half remember what had happened afterward, and yet there was *zero* question in my mind about whether we'd had sex. *Hello*, his dick was inside me, *obviously* we'd had sex! But with Sam, I was having some of the most intensely romantic, physically pleasurable sexual experiences of my life, we were falling in love, we would both come, and afterward I'd panic and say things like, "My freak virgin boyfriend won't have sex with me—I hate my life." I was more than a little misguided.

As time went by, we did begin to have penetrative sex. But by then we were so close, and so in tune with each other's body, that the "fucking" didn't change our sex life very dramatically. It didn't feel like: *Okay, now we're* actually *having sex, but before we weren't.* And even postdick, the fact that we couldn't do all the "standard" positions kept us creative. There was a lot of mouth work happening, and a lot of sticking weird stuff that we found lying around the house into my pussy (a flashlight, a teacup, whatever).

And sure, he might not have been bending me over tables to pound me, but I didn't mind, because while being table-railed is admittedly cinematic, it can be unnecessarily cruel to your cervix. And we got to do some other, equally cinematic things. Like the time when Sam spent three weeks in the hospital after an operation, and I would sneak into his room after visiting hours to resurrect our medical role play in an actual hospital bed. The faint smell of death added a weird vibe, but I accepted it as part of the authentic experience. I still credit those early, pervy medical exams for why even now, to this day, I often type "gynecologist" into the PornHub search bar. (But please don't repeat that.)

fucking outside the lines

Sam and I broke up when I was twenty-three. The sanitized version of the story is that we grew apart. The resentful version is that I grew into a sex blogger, and he was vaguely repulsed by that. (Oh, and I was also a bitchy unemployed unshowered ketamine addict, which might have factored into it.) But the relationship had piqued my interest in sex and disability—specifically, how disability can change the way a person has sex, or even the way they *define* sex. I wanted to learn more about it, and to hear people's stories. And so I did what any good investigative slut blogging autodidact would do: I spent all day on pervy sex forums, begging strangers to tell me their secrets.

One of my favorite interviews I did during that time

was with a twenty-five-year-old girl from New Jersey named Sarah, who I met on a forum for people who are into spanking. Sarah suffered from a rare form of dwarfism, was quadriplegic, and lived permanently on a ventilator. Because of her condition, for most of her life she'd had minimal contact with the outside world. However, in her late teens she discovered Second Life—you know, that early-2000s virtual world that's basically like the actual world, except you're allowed to fly and be a prostitute—after which she gave up "real life" almost completely. In SL Sarah had a successful career as a model, she was into kink and BDSM, and when I met her she was actively looking for a man to spend the rest of her life with. Through SL, she had created an existence for herself that did not rely on the capabilities of her body.

In the nonvirtual world, Sarah needed assistance with everything. She had enough movement in one hand to use a mouse, so she could utilize the internet by herself, but everything else required help, and because of that she'd accepted that having in-person sex with someone wasn't for her. But that didn't stop her from being a virtual ho. Through slutting around on SL, she'd worked out that she was sexually submissive, and described her taste as "sensual BDSM"—like, she enjoyed being tied up, but only if the guy was romantic about it. Once, she told me about losing her virginity, and how intensely emotional it had been for her. Hearing her describe the experience felt like hearing anyone describe what it's like to have sex for the first time. We actually ended up commiserating about how losing your virginity can be an anticlimax: I was complaining that the first guy I fucked only lasted fifteen seconds, and she was complaining that her guy used "poseballs" when he fucked her. Poseballs are a way of expressing yourself and touching on SL, but they're the way to touch someone that involves the least amount of effort. So her dude was basically the avatar equivalent of the guy who doesn't go down on you.

Clearly, before talking to Sarah, I would not have considered two avatars repeatedly crashing into each other a genuine sexual experience. But then I started to think: Why, though? If virtual fucking is the way that Sarah's body is capable of having and enjoying sex, then that's sex for her. If, as a society, we have been able to detach sex from its biblical purpose of procreation to redefine it as an activity between people that's done for sexual pleasure, then why does someone need to stick a dick into a vagina for "sex" to be *sex*?

Another one of my favorite interviews was with a woman named Pink, a then forty-two-year-old nanny from Seattle. Her boyfriend, Patrick, was a quadriplegic government employee. He didn't have feeling below his nipples and couldn't get an erection, but that didn't stop him from actualizing his inner sadist. Patrick had taken on Pink as his sex slave, and ordered her to abide by his house rules whenever they were together. Primarily, she had to be naked at all times, and was paid by him for her sexual services in jelly beans, and was only allowed ten jelly beans a day. Patrick had full range of motion in his arms, but both hands were stuck in fists. Whenever Pink deserved to be punished, Patrick would command her to slot a bamboo cane into his fist, which he could then swing in order to beat her. When Pink was well behaved, Patrick would allow her to put his fingers inside her while she masturbated—something she described as "heavenly." Together, they had conceived of an array of handy DIY contraptions, for instance, a machine that allowed for him to push a button that would trigger a paddle to hit her in the boob. Like all great partnerships, master-slave relationships rely on teamwork.

And then there was the blond bombshell Canadian sex worker I met last year, Bip. At the time, she worked for an organization called Sensual Solutions, which pairs sex workers with clients with physical impairments. One of her clients didn't have feeling below the waist, but through erotic coaching, together they were able to remap the erotic zones on his body so that he was literally able to achieve orgasm through her touching his earlobe. At first I assumed she was lying—like "I'm so good, I can make a man come through his ears" vibes—until I discovered that it's actually not that uncommon for a person with a spinal cord injury who's lost the ability to feel sensations in the genitals to develop new erogenous zones above the level of injury. I guess it's true what they say about orgasms being mostly mental.

Hearing all these stories made me realize how uncreative and lazy most of us can be when it comes to sex, unless we're literally forced to find new ways of being intimate with someone. Despite the endless ways that one person can make another feel good, so often we stick to the most basic solutions. It took a lot of hindsight for me to realize how special and significant those early sexual experiences with Sam were, and how oblivious I was for not considering them significant enough to be defined as sex.

The problem with our cultural definition of sex (essentially: dick in vagina) is that it delegitimizes the sexual experiences of people who can't have or aren't interested in having sex that way. That includes disabled people, most of the LGBTQ community, and, like, those people in Japan who get off on putting eels in women's vaginas or whatever. The traditional definition of sex also conflates being a man with having a penis and being a woman with having a vagina, but *hello*, it's 2018—we are now casually enlightened enough to know that not all women have vaginas. Basically, the way we think of sex is extremely dick-centric. And not only does dick define sex, dick also defines women. Women are consistently divided into two groups, virgins and nonvirgins, and the difference between those groups is a dick. Literally and figuratively.

fuck penetration

In his book *Sex Outside the Lines* (2015), sex therapist Dr. Chris Donaghue writes, "The concept of sex as penetration, with genitals as the tools, has vandalized the sexuality of all individuals.... We determine which body parts are sexual by social definition and socialization, and we prioritize specific procreative-based anatomy as sexual parts while illegitimizing the rest of the body. When pleasure, and not procreation, is the main goal of sex, the genitals are irrelevant, as erections and vaginal penetration are not required." Essentially, expanding our idea of sex would make it a lot less norm-y, and a lot more pleasurable, especially for women.

I probably sound like I'm super antidick right now, but I promise I'm not. Look, I like being fucked as much as the next guy. But there's a time and a place for everything. And in my opinion, penetration is a grossly overused resource.

So often, in straight sex, we stick to the most conventional itinerary: First some kissing, then groping and hand stuff, then the girl gives a BJ, maybe the guy gives some head, which all leads up to the main event—being pounded until the dick is satisfied. How boring. This might shock you, but you don't have to stick your dick in to have a good time. Penetration isn't necessary, and it's not always interesting. It's time to (literally) think outside the box.

We're so penetration obsessed that, in some people's minds, if you hook up with someone outside of your relationship, and do everything *except* stick your dick in, then it wasn't really cheating. *Right.* I was personally on the (non)receiving end of this theory back during my sugar baby epoch. One of my pretend boyfriends was a tall, tweedy Columbia professor in his midforties who was married with three kids. When he joined SeekingArrangement, he told himself that as long as he never stuck it in anyone, everything else was kosher. I told him that while I was happy to be an auxiliary to his self-manipulation, there was no way in hell that his wife would ever buy that as a valid excuse. He half agreed with me, but said he still needed to keep this rule for *himself*, otherwise his guilt would cock-block his fun, so to speak. (Again, I can't help but think of Joan Didion's famous adage: *We tell ourselves stories in order to live.*)

Of course, the idea that removing penetration somehow eliminates a level of closeness is totally insane. Conversely, it made my sexual interactions with the Professor arguably *more* intimate, because we ended up doing a lot more kissing and massage and tongue stuff, and a whole host of other playful, nonpounding activities. A lot more "foreplay," as it's often called. However, even the word "foreplay"—"fore" meaning "at the front of"—suggests that all nonpenetrative acts are just the appetizers, whereas penetration is the *goal* of sex. But maybe if we started to think of all intimate acts as equal, then we could actually slow down and enjoy the entire process more. When we focus solely on penetration, we forget about the pleasure of simply rubbing against someone.

And not fucking really heightens the sexual tension. In the heat of the moment, the Professor would always *almost* fuck me, but then would have a moral panic freakout and jump out of the bed—repeat to infinity. And eventually this became really frustrating for me, too. Usually during sex I wish guys would get more into foreplay, but when someone takes dick off the table, it's suddenly a hot commodity. Bizarrely, one of the hottest things about penetration is when you want it but can't have it. Basically, the moment when a woman is dying to be fucked is rare and precious—guys shouldn't be desperate, but they should be on call.

My new theory is that penetration should never be the beginning of sex, and we shouldn't automatically assume that it's the end of sex, either. Like, it's okay to fuck, then pull out for a while and go back to kissing or hand stuff or water sports or whatever you're into, and then come back to fucking again later on. Sticking to an itinerary is not sexy. But there *are* certain times when penetration is simply a NO. For instance, in the morning when I'm half-asleep and vaguely hungover and my mouth tastes like death, and the guy in my bed is trying to shove his penis into my desert vagina. It's like, "*Bro*, if you literally can't get it in, there's a reason—that's my pussy telling you to get the fuck away from me."

I actually wish more guys would get into pegging, because I think if men knew more about what it was like to get fucked, they would be better at fucking. The person doing the penetrating is the one in control, which means they have to be more aware of the other person—to observe their physical cues and gauge if they're feeling pleasure or if they're bored or suicidal. If you've never been fucked, you just can't be an expert in this department.

At this point it's no secret that most women can't orgasm from penetration alone. In fact, only 25 percent of women are consistently orgasmic during vaginal intercourse. In other words, dicks are not the magical orgasm wands their owners make them out to be. But still, in the years that I was with my girlfriend, it felt like literally once a week someone would ask me: "But don't you miss dick?" As if the penis is the holy grail of pleasure. As if dicks are the only dick-shaped things on earth. But as anyone who's ever thought about anything knows, hands and a mouth and toys can do everything that a dick can do— and far more. While the increasing cultural conversation around female pleasure has genuinely helped this issue— for instance, I'm pretty sure that most guys now realize that a woman can't come solely from deep-throating (even if she's having fun)—statistically, women who sleep with women still report having far more frequent orgasms during sex than women who sleep with men. Now, armed with my post-lesbian hindsight, I was a psycho for complaining about having a boyfriend who wasn't that interested in sticking it in.

is it even possible for lesbians to have sex, technically?

While lesbian sex might be an aphrodisiac for the male boner, it's also kryptonite for the male ego. This is why, when you're a woman dating another woman, you often have to put up with drunk guys asking you: "But wait, how do lesbians even have sex, anyway?" They're usually half-joking, half-serious. When I was with my girlfriend, I became so used to this question that I developed a stock response: "Oh, ya know, it's just like in lesbian porn," I'd say. "We sixty-nine wearing stilettos on the kitchen floor, and then after about five minutes our landlord comes in and fucks both of us."

Of course, this goes back to the "How do you define 'sex' as opposed to 'other stuff' when there's no dick involved?" question. In high school, I heard a variety of questionable answers to this conundrum: oral sex; fingering; some skater kid once told me, "It's not sex until you're knuckles deep," which in my teenage mind somehow seemed logical. To be fair, similar conversations arose about straight sex. Does anal sex count as sex? (Some Christians seem to think not.) If you give someone a blow job, have you had sex with them? The lines have long been blurry.

I have to admit, when I first started batting for team lez, I didn't *really* know the answer to this question, either. At the beginning of the relationship with my girlfriend, I was constantly worried that I was going to make some unknown lesbian faux pas, or that I was going to fuck "too straight" or something. I remember anxiously wondering: *Wait, is scissoring actually a thing, or just an ancient lesbian myth, passed down from porn generation to porn generation?* (Turns out, even lesbians don't know the answer to that question—I've asked almost all of them.)

Being with Alice made me feel like I was learning to have sex all over again (again). First of all, I learned that you *cannot* fake orgasms with girls. I swear, women have a sixth sense for telling when other women are faking it, even from like fifty feet away. With a dude, you can literally just be boiling pasta and then randomly say, "I'm coming," and he'll sincerely believe you. But with Alice, I could give an Oscar-winning performance and she would just laugh in my face. It's not like I was in the habit of faking it, but it's always comforting to know that you can fake it if you *need* to—like how you can cry yourself out of a speeding ticket, or blow-job yourself out of literally anything. Knowing I have it in my back pocket somehow enables me to relax during sex. But when you know you're going to be accountable for every fucking orgasm, you have to *actually* relax, which is clearly a recipe for anxiety.

But that was just a tiny part of the learning process. I also learned that when you're sleeping with someone who's genderqueer, there's sometimes literal body politics. When we started dating, Alice told me that she saw herself as falling somewhere in the middle of the gender spectrum— while she didn't identify as trans, or as a man, she didn't fully identify as a woman, either. And because of that, she said, she didn't really "relate to having a vagina." She didn't hate it, but she just saw herself as someone who had more of a metaphorical dick than a literal pussy, ya know? And because of that, she didn't like being penetrated. For the most part, she didn't even really like being touched down there. It was an iron-curtain situation.

Admittedly, this wasn't the easiest thing for me to wrap

my head around at first. The gender gray-area thing I understood. But not being able to touch her felt strange, like she was putting a wall up between us. For instance, she usually insisted on keeping her boxers on during sex. Outwardly, I tried to be chill about it, but in my head I was like, *God, what is it about* me *that makes people want to keep their clothes on while we fuck?!* Of course, the decision wasn't about *me*, it was about her and her sexual identity. But I'm a narcissist, so I don't think about other people.

So, if there's no boner and the vagina is off-limits, then what's left to do? Of course, we earlier addressed the option of building machinery to beat each other with, but neither Alice nor I was very handy. So we got creative in other ways. One of our favorite ways to fuck was for Alice to lie on top of me—generally her in her boxers and me naked—and then we'd intertwine our legs and basically just grind. And then after a while she'd start to fuck me with her fingers. This position was nice because it meant that basically our whole bodies could be touching at once, from our mouths to our toes. I Googled it, and the technical term for this is "frottage" (from the French word "to rub"—chic). It's surprisingly effective, and amazing if you're lazy and/or hungover. I guess you could say that this way of fucking was *our way*. But if you had asked me a handful of years earlier, I probably would have told you that *our way* didn't even count as sex.

Sometimes we'd do other stuff—like a strap-on situation, for instance. Despite my recent antidick rant, I'll admit that, after meeting Alice, one of the first things I did was go to a sex store and buy a large purple dildo and leather harness, because in my head I was like, *Well, this is what lesbians do, right?* I just felt like my new lesbian lover wouldn't take me seriously unless I had a fake dick in the house. But as it turned out, we only used the strap-on like five times in our three-year relationship, partly because it quickly dawned on me that I didn't need to imitate heterosexual sex in order to validate my queer sex. Rookie mistake. Also, Alice seemed to sort of resent the fact that, just because she wore boy's clothes and sometimes would refer to the size of her metaphorical dick (bigger than average, but not offensive), I would assume she had actual penis envy. My bad. Like, I remember this one time, she put on the strap-on, then immediately looked down and said, "Wait, I'm gay and dicks are weird. Why is this thing on me?"

Of course, wielding a purple plastic penis is not an affront to one's queerness, nor does it make you heteronormcore. After all, being queer isn't about hating dicks, and using a strap-on isn't about wanting to be a man (so if you were about to impulsively set your dildo on fire as a feminist performance art piece, you can just chill and keep reading instead). I know a lot of women who get off wearing a strap-on, either psychologically or because of the way it rubs against their clit. I know lesbians who, when they go on a Tinder date, will pack their penis in their bag—like that's *their dick.* There's no need to overintellectualize or overpoliticize it. If the point of sex is to create intimacy and to give and receive pleasure, then why restrict yourself from something that feels good just because of the patriarchy or whatever? If you ever wake up and realize that the patriarchy, dicks, or feminism is cramping your sex life, then it's time to reevaluate.

The point I'm trying to make is that sexuality is about intimacy, not intercourse. And for a committed slut and/ or slutty anthropologist, the goal should be to go into every sexual situation accepting it for what it is—the vast, complicated, often awkward, sometimes triggering, beautifully clumsy unknown.

what do i want?
chapter 7
hedonist or just immature?

My *greatest fear in life is being basic.* (Or, perhaps more accurately, regressing back into basicness.) I have a literal recurring nightmare where I wake up one day with a husband, two kids, and a house in the suburbs and can't remember how I got there, as if it's my *destiny*. To avoid this becoming a reality, my strategy thus far has been to continually destroy my relationships at the first sign that they're headed in that direction. So far, I have a 100 percent success rate with romantic sabotage.

I've had this kind of defiant reaction for years. At thirty-one, I've yet to live with a partner. Even in my one queer relationship, which was a welcome escape from the heteronormative default settings, as soon as my girlfriend initiated talk of buying a house together, I panicked and pulled away. I'm almost positive that I'm undeniably an adult now, but still, the idea of having a baby seems literally *bizarre* to me (like, where would I put it?). Of course, like most nonrobots, I want to form a loving and supportive bond with a hot person. But at the same time, I

suffer from a very serious disease known as Relationship
FOMO: As soon as I commit myself to one person, my
eggs start to panic, worried that they're missing out on
partying with cooler, smarter, more stylish sperm. It's a
constant struggle.

In some respects, I trust my instincts to avoid conventional relationship dynamics that I suspect won't make me
happy in the long run. But other times, I wonder if this
fear of normalcy is leading me to destroy valuable, loving
relationships simply to preserve some juvenile idea of rebellion. I question how practical it is to view life as one
endless hedonistic pursuit. Because the problem is, I really
like being in a relationship. It feels good to have consistent sex with someone who you don't hate. I mean, I don't
want to YOLO solo *forever*. And I think a lot of people
my age are wrestling with the same question: In order to
experience love and a lasting partnership, do you have to
close the chapter of your life that includes experimenta-
tion, spontaneity, and, well, freedom?

Recently, I was lamenting all of this to my therapist,
who's a very glamorous Upper East Side Jewish woman in
her sixties with a Susan Sontag–esque gray streak (so basically a cartoon shrink). I was giving her my usual rant—
something like "I'm kinda lonely, but having a boyfriend
makes me feel trapped, and oh my god am I a doomed
slut who's allergic to relationships and who's going to die
alone?!" et cetera. Usually she just nods silently, but this
time she said sternly, "Karley, *what do you want*? Don't
tell me what you think you deserve, or what you think

is realistic or fair. Tell me what you actually want, if you could have anything." And it was funny because I was like…*Wow, I don't know if I've ever truly asked myself that question*. I guess because I'm scared of the answer; I'm scared of sounding like a selfish, delusional egomaniac. The reality is, my dream is to be with someone who loves and respects me, who I deeply admire, who's smart and hot and loves giving head, but who also lets me occasionally have sex with a random, *and*—here's the kicker—who just naturally isn't interested in fucking anyone but me. Basically, I want to be free to let my slut flag fly while my partner stays locked in a cage. And that's the honest, unprogressive truth. When I told my therapist this, however, she literally cracked up. Like an actual LMAO moment. Should I take that as a sign that I'm being unrealistic?

To be honest, there's still a part of me that thinks, *It's fine! One day I'll just meet the one, I'll fall madly in love, and then I'll just naturally never want to fuck anyone else for the rest of my life.* And then there's this other part of me that's like, *You're delusional, ho.* Because if there's one thing I know about myself, it's that I'm not very good at saying no to something that I want—or more like, I don't *want* to say no. I'm supposed to feel guilty about that, right?

Certain people get off on sacrificing things for the sake of their relationship, but personally, self-sacrifice has often led me to resent my partner for preventing me from realizing all of my impulsive slutty desires (as if it was somehow their fault). Like, having a family seems cool, but then what if I meet two Louis Garrel look-alikes who invite me into an MMF threesome? I'm just supposed to pass? That's crazy. For a long time now, my sluttiness has been a fundamental part of my identity, and I don't want to lose that—but I also don't want to *just* be that. Some people argue that as we get older, we should naturally gain less of our life satisfaction and self-worth through sex, and instead get it from other sources, like our jobs and kids and vacation homes or whatever. But says who? What if I want to experience all the joys that love has to offer, but in forty years I also want to organize my first senior-citizen gang bang? What if I want to be a slut forever?

It's said that women reach our sexual peak in our thirties or even forties, whereas for men it's something awkward like sixteen. But growing up, I just felt so sure that my twenties would be the pinnacle of my sex life—the decade when I would be the most adventurous and cellulite-free, which would naturally translate to having the best sex. (Paradoxically, I still believed this well into my midtwenties, a period when I repeatedly made the analogy that having penetrative sex felt like inserting a tampon over and over.) At thirty, I figured, things start to sag, you become a boring adult, and your sex life takes a back seat until eventually, at forty-five-ish, you switch off your uterus, buy a minivan, and sew your vagina shut forever. But since age sixteen, the pleasure I get from sex has been on a steady incline. I come more often and in more positions. I have more sexual confidence and have earned enough self-regard to avoid ending up in bed with total assholes. Today, I generally walk away from sexual encounters feeling happy and satisfied rather than limping away feeling like my vaginal walls have just endured target practice. It's a nice place to be, honestly.

I think part of the reason sex keeps getting better is that when I was younger, I felt like I needed to be a lot more performative during sex—like I needed to put on a show for whatever random bar stranger ended up in my bed that night. As women, we're inundated with ideals for our physical presentation—from SoulCycle-ing our thighs into shape to spending $300 on a bra that promises to defy gravity. And of course it can be fun to play with all the trappings of the feminine aesthetic. However, there's a difference between drawing a flirty cat eye and turning every sexual encounter into a drunken cabaret moment, giving blow jobs in a fucking backbend and waking up with a kink in my neck, and never once factoring my own sexual pleasure into this deranged sex theater. Pretty much across the board, my sexual experiences were plagued with me thinking: *Do I look hot enough? Does my face look like the girl from* The Ring *when I come? Do I need to bleach my butthole?!* And honestly I still have those thoughts during sex—especially the butthole one—but they're less frequent, and I'm better at shoving them out of my mind in order to think about more pertinent things (like prison gang-bang porn). As I grow up, I just naturally give less of a fuck. And it's so freeing. But annoyingly, the moment when we hit our sexual stride often coincides with the moment in our lives that we're told "Okay, honey, you've had fun, but it's time to settle down."

There seems to be a logical solution to all of this: If you suck at monogamy and want to continue on your slutty journey, then just be in an open relationship, duh! All you have to do is form a resilient bond with someone who you love and respect, never get jealous when they rail other people, ignore all basic societal expectations, and just casually be an enlightened sexual pioneer. Problem solved! Also, while you're at it, maybe win the Nobel Prize, lose ten pounds, and stop blacking out every night. Cool—I'll get right on that.

For all the obvious tortures of monogamy, non-monogamy comes with a whole other set of issues. For one, it's not that easy to find people who want to date a total ho. See, there's this idea floating around in the universe that when you truly love someone, you don't want to fuck other people. Clearly, that's insane. I, for one, have been deeply in love and still wanted to deep-throat the waiter. But people don't like this version of a love story—especially when you're dating them. And then there's the jealousy issue, to which I am not immune. Like, I consider myself a pretty sane person, but I've also been known to go full Lorena Bobbitt at the inkling my partner has a crush. Being a jealous slut is a dangerous and inconvenient combination.

And beyond the interpersonal issues, there's also a huge social stigma to nonmonogamy. Like, when you tell people you're in an open relationship, they usually look at you like you're a fucking idiot. And then laugh condescendingly and say something like: "So you *actually* think an open relationship can work long term?" To this, my response is: "Well, do you actually think a *monogamous* relationship can work long term?" This usually shuts them up—or at least throws them off for a few seconds.

It's true: Nonmonogamy is complicated, and making it work requires serious effort. But isn't the same true for monogamy? I'm sorry, but the idea that fucking only *one person* for the majority of your life is in any way "easy" is simply a joke. It's funny: When it comes to our professional lives, we admire people who value freedom. I'm proud that I'm my own boss, that I've never had a mundane office job, and that I can work from home or pack up and write from a beach for a month if I want to. For the most part, I'm not beholden to anyone, and each day is a unique experience full of new and interesting people. And people respect that. And yet, when we desire the same thing from our relationships—autonomy, freedom, and diversity—people are like, "Yeah, you're kind of a selfish asshole." What gives?

Deep down, I understand that if I want to form a (somewhat) stable long-term partnership with someone who I don't quickly grow to resent, it's likely going to have to be an open arrangement of some sort—perhaps only to a slight degree, and perhaps after a foundational period of monogamy, but the *possibility* needs to be there. The problem is, after years of trying, I'm still in the dark about how to make an open relationship—my romantic holy grail—not spiral into a total disaster.

sluts have more headaches

My first attempt at nonmonogamy was while I was living in London, soon after my relationship with Sam ended. I was twenty-three, and fell really hard for this beardy Scottish musician. He lived in Glasgow but came to London a couple of times a month with his band. I met him while high on ecstasy at a squat rave, obviously. Our dangerously dilated eyes met from across the puke-covered factory floor, and I walked straight up to him and, without saying a word, grabbed his dick through his pants. I guess that's sexual assault—but it worked.

We started dating, and it was one of those intense, voraciously sexual romances where you fuck like five times a day and spend full weekends without leaving the bed. He was gross in all the best ways. Once, I got my period while we were having sex, and instead of being disgusted he just reached down, grabbed a handful of blood, shoved it into my mouth, and then violently made out with me. I was like…"Wait, are you *the one*?"

If we'd lived in the same city we would have been inseparable. However, since we only saw each other a couple of times a month, and because we were both quite "sexually curious" (to put it lightly), we decided to date, but keep it "loose." This meant that when we were together we were *together*, but when we were apart we could do whatever we wanted. And this worked wonderfully for a while. We both felt confident about how much we liked each other, which meant that neither of us was worried about the other falling in love with a random second-tier fuck. Also, since we lived in different cities, our extracurricular sex lives were clearly separate from each other—I didn't have to know the girls he was banging or worry about running into them at parties, and vice versa. Out of sight, out of mind. And then, whenever we were in the same place, we would have missed each other so much that our time together would be super sexually charged and lovey-dovey. We once even had a conversation (while high, clearly) about how fucking other people often acted as a reminder of how much we cared about each other, because no one else matched up. It was the perfect combo of sexual freedom and romantic companionship, minus the all-too-common "If you fuck someone else I'll chop your dick off" component.

But then, about six months into our love affair, he moved from Glasgow to London. Cue the downward spiral. Suddenly, the fact that he was sleeping with other people was in my face, which clearly made it a lot harder to hair-flip from my consciousness. I remember once, a couple of weeks after his move, I was at a small party at his squat (he lived in a squat like five minutes' walk from my squat—romantic) and one of his "friends" from university came to visit him, a pretty, raven-haired Scottish girl who I instantly wanted to skin alive. He took me aside and explained that this girl was just a friend with benefits and not an actual threat. But still, I felt like there was an actual knife being twisted in my side. It was the first time I had to deal with the harsh reality that, when you're in an open relationship, sometimes your partner is going to make the choice to be with someone else over you. And you're not allowed to throw a fucking tantrum, because those are the rules of the game.

Now, clearly, every open relationship is different, and people are free to set the rules and boundaries that make them feel the most happy and sane. I admit that during this first attempt at being open, I was young and naive to the whole nonmonogamy thing, and didn't understand that openness is a constant negotiation, and in theory you should never have to feel like you're being stabbed in the uterus. Maybe I could have salvaged that relationship if I had been better at talking about what extracurricular activities I could handle, versus what types of situations would trigger a jealousy vortex. But instead of trying to rectify the situation, I just bailed. *Sigh*. If it weren't for romantic jealousy, being human would be so much more chill.

A few years later, about a year into dating Max (and about six months into our exclusivity), I experimented with being in an open relationship for a second time. This time we weren't sleeping with people independently of each other, but together we decided that it would be fun to try a threesome…or two or seven. The first time was really great. We'd finally hit a stride in our relationship— for as psychologically morbid as it was at times, this was a high point, and I felt really in love—so when we invited over one of our sort-of friends for the evening, it felt like something we were really doing *together*. Leading up to the evening, it was fun to cofantasize about what would happen, and who was going to tie her up and spit in her mouth or whatever. Once the girl was in bed with us, the whole evening felt really playful and sexy, and afterward it provided fodder for dirty talk for weeks to come. Because I was confident in our relationship, it felt fun and freeing to be like, "Fuck societal standards, I'm the Indiana Jones of sluts!" Ya know, cliché sexual self-discovery stuff.

After that, we were on a threesome upswing. We had a sexy MDMA shower with a busty French TV producer. We dildoed an ex-stripper while she was on the phone with her mom. We fucked my intern against a chain-link fence. It was all very glamorous. And finding people to bang was so bizarrely easy. Our tactic was literally to just text the girl of our choosing: *Hey, wanna get threesomed?* Somehow this strategy was almost infallible.

But then, about a year after our first ménage, the relationship started to go downhill. Not because of the group sex, more because Max too often Dr. Jekylled into a verbally abusive, tyrannical version of himself, which in turn made me behave like a noodly, needy, insecure mess. I felt newly insecure in our relationship—primarily, about his commitment to it—and suddenly the thought of watching him fuck someone else no longer seemed "team building." If I were smarter and stronger, I would've admitted this to him and explained why I didn't think it was a good idea to group-bang someone while our relationship was on the fritz, and while I was in a state of emotional dynamite. But instead, I chose to make the same mistake I did in my first go at nonmonogamy: to just fake a smile (and an orgasm or two) and zombie-walk through the flames.

There was this moment during that last threesome when I was watching him bang this girl—one of his ex–fuck buddies—and I saw them having this private moment of connection, and I felt like I was going to literally puke. And maybe he should have been more sensitive to my feelings, but at the end of the day, I'd put myself in that position (again). Turns out, our partners can't read our minds, and being a passive-aggressive cunt doesn't always communicate the subtle nuances of our feelings. I guess that's why we hear, ad nauseum, that the key to a healthy relationship is communifuckingcation. And that's even more true when your relationship involves a rotating cast of blow-job guest stars.

But third time's a charm, right? Lol, no. My third go at nonmonogamy was at twenty-seven, with Alice. She and I met just after I'd left my two-plus-year relationship with Max, and she had just ended an even longer relationship with a woman. For obvious reasons, both of us were hesitant to commit to something restrictive right away. But we really liked each other, so I suggested we keep things open—because, ya know, I'm *super* progressive, and because I'd had *so* much success with it in the past.

As usual, in the beginning it was great: I had a loving partner to have dinner and feelings-y sex with, but I was still allowed the occasional hookup with guys from the post office or internet or wherever. Plus, I had *just* started working as a sugar baby at the time, and I didn't want to give that up (for financial reasons, but also because I had the foresight to understand it would one day be glamorous to drop "Back when I was a prostitute…" casually at a dinner party). Being open meant that I didn't have to bail on that perverted dream. It was the best of both worlds. Of course, even in the beginning I would sometimes get jealous of Alice's affairs. Let's be real, even in my most open-minded mood, the thought of her banging someone else made me want to pull a Left Eye and burn down her apartment. But these fleeting moments of violent rage felt like a small price to pay for my sexual freedom. And the fact that I was able to rationalize that—that I was willing to sacrifice the pain for the gain—made me feel like this time around I might have matured enough to make nonmonogamy work long term.

But then something happened that I wasn't expecting: We got competitive. Basically, if my girlfriend went on a date, my wounded ego obliged me to do the same, so as not to fall behind. Suddenly, our peripheral sex lives seemed to be just as much about payback as they were about pleasure. A fuck for a fuck, if you will. And that wasn't the only problem. There was also the fact that when we'd decided to be open, we hadn't really set any ground rules, aside from, like, "Don't fall in love with anyone else." But as time went on, and as we started ending up in situations where one of us felt betrayed, we were suddenly faced with the question: How *open* is open? Does open mean a no-boundaries slutfest in which both partners are free to form secondary relationships and show up to dinner covered in a stranger's cum? Or does it mean that very occasionally, when an extracurricular hookup happens, you both just force a smile and pray no one got herpes?

Over time we worked out our boundaries and set rules that made sense for us. For instance: no sleeping with mutual friends, no sleepovers, no "regulars," and no banging someone else within an hour of hanging out with each other (an obvious sacrifice, but one I was willing to make for true love). We stayed open for nine months, which felt pretty successful. But then disaster struck, in the worst way: She fell for one of her fuck buddies and started secretly dating her—the thing slutty nightmares are made of.

Here's the super-condensed version of what happened: Basically, even though Alice had agreed to be in an open relationship, I was definitely the one who, shall we say, "utilized my privileges" more frequently. After a while, this imbalance started to make her secretly resentful. Then she started banging a woman who I'll refer to simply as the Cunt (to this day, I consider her my archnemesis). So, the Cunt becomes obsessed with Alice and gives her a ton of love and attention, and suddenly Alice feels very drawn to the Cunt because she's giving her all the affection that she feels is lacking in our relationship. Alice then ends up secretly spending the entire Thanksgiving weekend with the Cunt, while I'm upstate with my family. I discovered this through the very classy and high-tech tactic known as "looking at her phone while she's in the shower." Predictably, I had a mental breakdown and gave her an ultimatum: stop railing the Cunt and be monogamous with me, or we're over. She chose me (but mainly, I think, because my level of manic rage rendered her literally scared for her life).

For the next two years we were monogamous, and pretty successful at it—aside from that time she cheated on me (with the Cunt) and then I cheated on her back with a lesbian Mormon pornographer...but whatever, no one's perfect. Monogamy certainly wasn't easy, but I was really in love, and the sacrifice felt unquestionably worth it to me. And while it's off brand for me to be sincere, I will say that, during those two years, being with her made me feel so loved and safe and supported and happy. She was unquestionably *my person*. But of course, there's an expiration date to any diet, and almost two years to the day from when we closed our relationship, I pressured her to open it again.

This time, we barely lasted two months before the relationship imploded. I've intentionally blocked out a lot of the details, but let's just say that one evening, I locked myself in the bathroom with Alice's phone, went onto her Tinder account, found all the phone numbers of the girls she had slept with, put their numbers into *my* phone, and then proceeded to send all of them threatening text messages in the vein of *If you ever text my girlfriend again I'll fucking kill you!! I KNOW WHERE YOU LIVE!* Yeah, definitely a low point for me. Not surprisingly, we broke up very soon after that. Post-violent-Tinder-meltdown, I got to thinking: What the fuck does it take to make an open relationship work?

the (ethical) slutty basics

Embarking on a quest for the perfect slutty relationship has become increasingly fashionable in recent years. In fact, people have built entire careers out of trying to conquer Pandora's slutty box. The aforementioned sex writer and podcaster Dan Savage is an active proponent of what he calls "monogamish"—"opening the door of your relationship just a crack, to keep it from blowing off its hinges," as he puts it. Dossie Easton and Janet Hardy's book *The Ethical Slut*—probably the quintessential guide to nonmonogamy—has been selling consistently since its publication in 1997. And then there's *Sex at Dawn*, Christopher Ryan and Cacilda Jethá's 2010 bestseller, which argues that monogamy goes against human nature. The book's enormous popularity spawned countless articles and debates about whether monogamy is in fact a social construct, and one that goes against our biology. All of this demonstrates an increasing cultural interest in relationships that deviate from the norm of monogamy.

But just because something is trendy doesn't mean that it's easy, and just because something feels idyllic and like it "makes sense in the long run" doesn't mean that it won't drive you fucking mental. Like, I rationally understand that if I didn't drink a bottle of Prosecco every night, I would be skinnier and less of a hungover maniac, but that doesn't make me order seltzer. And I know that if I could curb my jealousy and offer my partner the same freedoms that I seek for myself, I would be more likely to form a relationship that didn't feel like a prison cell. *Sigh*. If only knowing things meant something.

Nonmonogamous relationships generally fall into one of three main categories: swinging, polyamory, and open relationships. Swingers are the most couple-centric of the three—these are lovers in a committed relationship who have strictly casual sex with other people, which they typically engage in together, at a swingers' party or some other "lifestyle" event. Open relationships are similar in that a committed couple can have casual hookups, but their extracurricular sex tends to happen independently. These couples will usually create specific boundaries based on their personal comfort levels—for instance, a "no sleepovers" rule, or an "area code" rule. Finally, polyamory refers to people who have multiple simultaneous relationships that are not just sexual, but emotional and romantic as well. For instance, one could have a primary partner and a secondary partner, or three or four people could all be romantically linked together, known as a triad or a quad, respectively.

An open relationship seems like the best option for me, mainly because I prefer my extracurricular sex to happen solo, as in not at a sex party surrounded by a bunch of people who look like they were born and raised at Burning Man. Also, if my partner is going to be railing someone else, I'd rather not be present, thanks. Also, being poly just sounds way too time consuming. Like, I can't even find time to pick up my laundry, let alone massage both of my boyfriends' egos and prostates. There's only so many orgasms in the day.

Beyond freedom and transparency, there are some other, more hidden perks to nonmonogamy. For example, it's well-known poly lore that a primary virtue of being open is that it prevents you from getting lazy or taking each other for granted—the slight competition keeps you engaged and motivates you to win each other's affection every day. So basically, if you're open, your husband is less likely to get a beer gut. And there's also the issue of honesty. Let's not kid ourselves: Adultery is rife. In a way, the social norm of monogamy requires a certain degree of dishonesty. It's almost like monogamous couples actually *prefer* to be lied to rather than deal with the uncomfortable reality of extra-relationship attraction.

I currently have two close friends in successful long-term nonmonogamous relationships, so I've seen first-hand that it does really work for some people. The first is Anna, a law professor who's been in an open marriage for seven years with an extremely sweet businessman. Anna's from Macedonia, or one of those other weird Eastern European countries where people don't have feelings, which I assume is a primary reason why she never seems to care when her husband brings one of his many side hos on a sexy beach vacay. (Technically, people from Eastern Europe are a little bit less human than the rest of us.) Anna is an extreme case. For one, she's thirty-four and has already slept with more than a thousand people. That's pretty impressive—on a physical level, but also just logistically. I'm stressed just thinking about her iCal. One of Anna's hobbies is organizing gang bangs for herself and her friends. I found this out after I once casually mentioned that I like Public Disgrace, the kinky gang-bang porn series, to which Anna responded, "OMG, I throw gang bangs! Let me know if you're interested and I can *totally* make that happen for you!" Now, every couple of months or so I get a text from her like, *Hey, just putting together another GB. Let me know if you want in, babe!* Followed by the salsa-dancing emoji.

It's clear that Anna and her husband really love each other. While I would literally rather die than engage in their extreme level of double-penetration polymania, I really respect what they've created. They're a perfect example of the fact that, as long you and your partner both want the same thing, you can make literally any type of relationship work—even one that lets you take ten dicks at a time on a random Wednesday.

My other nonmonogamous friend is Colette. She's a thirty-five-year-old dominatrix with a PhD in psychology, and for the last four years she's been in a polyamorous relationship with her boyfriend, Dan, a thirty-seven-year-old tech millionaire. (Yes, they live in Berkeley—you guessed right.) I've gone to visit them multiple times, and even though I'm not trying to be poly specifically, their relationship is closer to something I would want for myself. Put simply, they're both super-hot, successful, rich, smart, and kinky; they're clearly very in love; and yet they offer each other the freedom to fuck and care about other people. (Annoyingly, neither of them has ever tried to have sex with me, which I'm offended by, honestly.)

During one of my visits to their Berkeley mansion, I had something of a slutty lightbulb moment, which I once wrote about for *Vogue*. Until then, I always knew that nonmonogamy had the specific benefit of allowing you to continue your sexual exploration, even while being in a supportive relationship, or after marriage or whatever. But seeing Colette and Dan's home life made me realize that outside of the obvious sexual perks, nonmonogamy lays the groundwork for a genuinely unique and thrilling lifestyle, in ways far beyond novelty fucks. Being non-monogamous is, essentially, the opposite of being basic.

When I arrived at Colette and Dan's beautiful hilltop home on a Saturday morning in the spring of 2016, Dan answered the door wearing silk pajama pants. "Colette's in the orgy room, meditating," he said with a smile. They'd hired a rent-a-shaman to come up from Mexico that afternoon, to dose a handful of their friends with a psychoactive toad venom containing the powerful hallucinogen 5-MeO-DMT, known to induce divine revelation or, in Colette's words, "ego death." (Think ayahuasca but without the puking.) I was there in part to "observe" Colette and Dan's relationship dynamic—sort of like being on a poly safari—and in part to try to see if this magical toad could collaborate with the slut gods to miraculously solve all my relationship problems. Or something.

With a few hours to kill before the ceremony, Colette invited me to one of her dominatrix sessions to watch her electrocute a man's balls. How could I say no? So after breakfast we all hopped into Dan's self-driving Tesla and headed to Colette's dungeon. Watching their morning exchange made me smile—they talked about planning a trip to see Dan's family, and Dan made Colette oatmeal as she packed her Prada bag full of latex lingerie and washed her dildos in the sink. It was cool to see how they'd forged a relationship that is at once loving and domestic but also completely unorthodox. It's like, just because you're polyglamorous and host chic orgies doesn't mean you don't make breakfast and hang with each other's mom, ya know? I kept thinking: That—*that's what I want*.

Still, they're the first to admit that defying convention is no walk in the park. "It's really not easy to be in a poly relationship," Colette told me as the robot car drove us to her dungeon. "You're allowing yourself to be thrown into situations that can arouse feelings of jealousy, insecurity, neediness—emotions you always thought you would avoid at all costs." But ultimately, she prefers a relationship that's challenging to one that's binding. "That traditional relationship model just doesn't work for me at all," she said. "Plus, it feels good to carve out your own type of relationship. The idea of doing what everyone else does just feels insane to me."

"People seek monogamy and 'till death do us part' because it gives them security," Dan added. "They want to believe that the other person is never going to run off. But Colette and I both value our freedom to explore life in an unbounded fashion, and to love and to build relationships with many people. Within the open relationship, what makes Colette so special to me is that I learn more from her and I evolve quicker with her than I have with any other woman."

"In all my previous relationships, my partners said I was 'too much,'" Colette recalled. "With Dan, we obviously have issues that we have to work through, but I'm so happy to finally be with someone who radically accepts me for me: a weird, polyamorous sex worker." The key, they both agreed, is not entering a relationship with someone who's fundamentally trying to make you more normal than you want to be. And that is certainly a mistake I've made ad nauseum. Over the years, I have repeatedly found myself in relationships with people who loved me, but who were basically like: "So it's cool that you're a professional sex maniac or whatever, but now that we're together, can you, ya know…tone it down?" (Like, I once had a guy I was dating introduce me to his family by saying that I wrote *Vogue*'s "emotional health column." I was like, "*Sex column*, it's a *sex column*, bro. My last article was about how I masturbate thinking about Anthony Weiner. That is emotionally healthy for no one.") Either that, or I've dated sex maniacs who were "too much" *for me*. The goal, I suppose, is finding that special partnership where we're both "just enough" for each other. I'm basically slutty Goldilocks, except swap out porridge for…I don't know, cum? That's gross, sorry.

It's clear that, underneath all the openness of Colette and Dan's relationship, they have a very strong base level of security—and that's essential when your partner is regularly spending Saturday evenings inside another human being. It can't be easy to say, "Have fun at the orgy, honey," if you suspect your partner might leave you for one of the fluffers. Colette told me, "People are afraid of non-monogamy because they're scared that the person they love is going to run away from them. But that fear is based on insecurity. You have to be able to love and accept yourself. Because ultimately I know that if Dan finds someone who he's more compatible with, I'm going to be fine. It won't be *easy*, but I will be okay. So you kind of have to be okay with the idea that your partner might run off—it's always a possibility, but that's also true of monogamous relationships." She shrugged nonchalantly. "My analogy is that if you have a dog in your yard, you can make the choice to put a fence around it, or you can let him run free, and if he keeps coming back to you, that's how you truly knows he loves you—and yes, I am comparing men to dogs in this analogy."

I asked Colette if she ever felt the desire (or the pressure) to have kids. "Recently," she said, "Dan and I were on acid, and we were laughing and having this amazing time, and then suddenly I had this thought, like, 'Wait, if we had kids, it would *ruin everything*. Everything we've been working for—our freedom—would be destroyed." She thought for a moment. "We're on this earth to make things. Some people choose to make babies. Others choose to write books or make films or start a company. We're not leaving our genes behind, but we're leaving a different kind of imprint."

I respect the practicality of that. In recent years, the

Sheryl Sandberg brand of lean-in feminism has been promoting the old "you can have it all" narrative again—you can be a "girl boss" at work, *and* have a romantic and intellectual partnership, *and* raise precocious little mini-me's *all* at the same time. It's like, okay, sure, but what if you're not rich enough to have a maid? And what if you don't want your kid to be raised by a nanny? And what if you love spending your weekday evenings alone, smoking weed and Googling "Jon Hamm penis" for five hours? At some point, something's gotta give.

I understand that I can't just shrug off the significance of having a family simply because it feels conventional to me, or because I think it will interfere with my rigorous masturbation schedule. I understand that major life steps like having kids, getting married, and buying a house fulfill basic human necessities: People want to be part of a community; we want to feel appreciated and secure; we don't want to spend middle age alone, eating canned tuna and being casually racist on Reddit. And the older I get, the more I admittedly feel drawn to these conventional landmarks. Like, if you had asked me two years ago about having a family, I would have been like, "Eww, why would I have kids when I could devote my life to more important things, like blogging and attending mediocre sex parties?" But now I'm like, "I'm too lazy to go out. Maybe I should just start a family." (I guess biology is real?)

But I try to remind myself there are other, less traditional ways of fulfilling these fundamental human desires. Maybe those of us living outside the lines have to create our own milestones—you make your first movie, you buy an apartment with your girlfriend, you sell a painting, you run a marathon, you redecorate your house, you go traveling, you write a book about being a slut that will make it ten times harder to ever get a boyfriend, et cetera. Maybe you don't have your own kids, but you adopt a proxy family of drag queens. Maybe you foster dogs. Maybe you start a brothel and the prostitutes act as your surrogate children. Maybe you don't get married, but you acquire a devoted sex slave who sleeps in a cage in your attic. The point is, love and security take many forms, the unconventional of which are often harder to see, which makes it all the more exciting to discover them.

sex is so perfect. why destroy it with a relationship?

When I was a kid, I had an image in my head of what a "good relationship" looked like, based mainly on my favorite sappy rom-coms and what I gleaned from the relationships of my parents and their friends. I remember "inseparable" being a word people often used positively when describing relationships—"they're inseparable" was another way of saying "they're very in love." I imagined a good boyfriend as a guy who would come with me to my friend's birthday party without complaining. This is pretty standard thinking. Romantic relationships are informed by all kinds of socially sanctioned ideas about what is a normal and good way to express your love for another person. Generally, this translates to: someone who will always be at your side. But isn't that a depressingly simplistic way to define love and connection? Shouldn't an ideal relationship be two people who support and understand each other, rather than two people who stand next to each other by default?

In her bestselling book *Mating in Captivity* (2006), famed psychotherapist Esther Perel describes how maintaining space, independence, and individual goals is essential to sustaining the allure of your partner over time. Perel's research shows that across cultural, religious, race, and gender lines, people report being most drawn to their partners when they are away—when they are able to long for each other and then reunite—or when their partner is doing something they are passionate about—when they're onstage, in the studio, in their element, when they are radiant and self-sustaining. When, suddenly, the person we know so well becomes once again mysterious and elusive. Putting it frankly, Perel says, "Fire needs air. Desire needs space."

If there's one thing I've learned about myself thus far in my adult dating life, it's that I need a lot of space. Like, acres. Sometimes I worry it will never be enough. Like, how am I supposed to share a life with someone when I can't even bring myself to share a bathroom? (I'm sorry, but I don't need someone else's shampoo all up in my shampoo. I have enough anxiety.) Even in my open relationship, where I was given a ton of freedom, I still found myself bending the rules almost compulsively. And now I'm like, *Shit... at what point do I have to stop blaming society for all my problems, and actually admit that the problem just might be* me? *Do I just suck at relationships?*

Despite all my commitmentphobia and boundary issues, to my credit, there is one type of relationship that I have mastered: the fuck buddy. I'm *really* good at fuck buddies. To me, fuck buddies feel like this weird life hack where you get to be close to someone and have sex semi-regularly while offering them literally nothing. As it turns out, I'm great at that! When it comes to offering people nothing, I'm extremely passionate and consistent.

It's telling that the two longest relationships of my life have both been with men who I was never officially dating. The first guy, Ben, was my friend with benefits for eight years. We met when I lived in London, when I was twenty-two and he was seventeen (that's legal there, I checked). For most of that time we lived on different continents, but inevitably, a couple of times a year, we'd find each other somewhere in the world, have a few days of romance, and then go our separate ways. And while I couldn't imagine being with Ben "for real"—I mean, he's a low-key homeless anarchist who once took me on a date to his Sex and Love Addicts Anonymous meeting; there are red flags—I still valued our relationship immensely. I mean, *eight years*, that's longer than I predict my first marriage will last. And honestly, Ben knows me better than a lot of my partners ever did.

People are skeptical of fuck buddies. They're like: How

can you have sex with the same person, again and again, without falling in love? Or at least, without getting super jealous and *Fatal Attraction*–esque? Some assume that one of the "buddies" is always being strung along, secretly hoping that the fucking leads to something more serious. Others dismiss fuck-buddy dynamics as just being compulsive sex that's devoid of emotion. But I beg to differ. For me, this dynamic has been a way to have a relationship while removing the creepy ownership of another human being. Fuck buddies have felt like the perfect middle ground: a liminal space between so-called eternal love and zombie-fucking a stranger; a place where you can care about someone, have good sex, and yet not want to literally implode at the thought of them sleeping with someone else.

Case in point: The most significant romantic friendship of my life, Malcolm, my aforementioned editor who helped me harness my slut powers. When Malcolm and I met, we bonded over our shared ineptitude at "normal" dating. He would always tell me, "Sex is so perfect. Why destroy it with a relationship?" I'm pretty sure it was meant as a joke, at least partially, but it left a nagging imprint on my dating subconscious.

In the years since we first met, there have been times when Malcolm and I saw each other frequently, and other times when things dropped off for a while, usually because one of us had a partner. And sure, when he would get a girlfriend, I'd be a little bummed out, but it didn't cause me to spiral into an emotional cyclone the way I would have if I'd been cheated on by a boyfriend. After all, disappointment comes from expectation. Ironically, when my fuck buddies tell me stories about their crazy and hot sex adventures, I can get really turned on. I can't count the number of times I've touched myself while in bed with a fuck buddy, listening to them detail the time they were willingly statutory-raped by one of their friend's moms. But when my partner talks about people they've fucked, all hell breaks loose. Why is that?!

Over time, Malcolm and I became intensely close—in a sex way, but also in a friend way. It felt like we had entered this secret bubble of transparency—we were emotionally intimate, yet free of the burden of jealousy and ownership. We could spill our guts to each other because we didn't have anything to lose. I told Malcolm about my previous relationships, my heartbreak, and my likely problematic predilection for porn where the sex looks slightly painful for the woman (not my fault—I didn't program myself). It seems counterintuitive, but at times it has been easier for me to be more open and honest with friends with benefits than with my actual partners. This paradox always makes me think of that *Mad Men* episode where Betty seduces Don at their kids' summer camp, well after they'd both remarried. Afterward, when they're lying in bed together, Betty says of Don's new wife, "That poor girl. She doesn't know that loving you is the worst way to get to you." Harsh. But sometimes romantic friendships can offer a type of intimacy that committed relationships can't.

I recently brought all of this up with Malcolm. He told

me, "Having a friend with benefits is great because it's just—it's just less *annoying*. It's more of a low-intensity intimacy. It's not encumbered by obligations, which just lead to resentment. We are all selfish—we all live in this Ayn Rand–ish self-centered world, whether we like it or not. When you're in a friends-with-benefits situation, you don't have to go to the other person's awful friend's birthday party. But if you behave like that within a conventional relationship, it causes problems." In other words, your fuck buddy gets all the good stuff about being in a relationship—the wild sex, the cuddles, the juicy dark secrets—minus all the boring, would-rather-die activities that go hand in hand with commitment, like having to help assemble your boyfriend's IKEA bed, or having to watch your girlfriend stab at the ingrown hairs on her bikini line while she watches the Kardashians. (That's me—I'm the girlfriend who does that.)

Honestly, sometimes I ask myself: *Why do I feel like I need a long-term live-in partner, anyway? Why is it weird to think that my friends with benefits could satisfy my need for intimacy and connection for the rest of my life, while leaving me all the space I need to fuck strangers for blog anecdotes?* It seems kind of chic to be a woman whose life includes an ever-changing rotation of new and diverse lovers. There's a part in the film *The Royal Tenenbaums* where a montage shows the many suitors of Etheline Tenenbaum (Anjelica Huston) over her life, ranging from archaeologists to writers to Arctic explorers. Whenever I watch it I think, *Wow, that's so glamorous—maybe* that's *what I want!* Imagine how much I could grow and learn and how dynamic my life could be if I were constantly being energized by new blood. At the same time, perhaps the reason romantic friendships have always been so attractive to me is that they lack the soul-baring vulnerability and intense emotional investment that are integral to a more committed partnership. And it would be silly of me not to think that I could learn a lot from that dynamic, too.

a slutty future

Not long ago, I was emailing back and forth with Christopher Ryan, author of *Sex at Dawn*, about my never-ending relationship-versus-freedom anxiety. (Really, he's the best friend to have when you need advice about your slutty problems.) I was explaining to him that, yet again, I had found myself deeply in crush with a guy who didn't seem very interested in nonmonogamy, and I couldn't help but think: *Wait, why am I back here* again? *Why am I investing my time in yet another person who doesn't want what I want?* Chris's response was so perfect. He wrote me:

> For what it's worth, my life changed dramatically when I started offering people only what I had to offer, as opposed to what I knew they wanted. I thought I was entering a romantic/sexual desert, but it ended up closer to a fucking Gauguin painting. I know it's harder for women (because men can be so narrow-minded), but things got A LOT

easier for me once I adopted a "this-is-who-I-am,
take-it-or-leave-it" approach to all things romantic.
It eliminates all the time wasted in cultivating relationships destined to hit the wall of truth
eventually—and the ensuing suffering. Better to filter them out early and invest that time in people
who are interested in who we REALLY are. Plus,
that has the added benefit of helping us work out
who the fuck we are, too.

So good, right? It reminds me of what Colette said
about Dan: "I'm so happy to finally be with someone
who radically accepts me for me: a weird, polyamorous
sex worker." And I guess that is ultimately what I want. I
want to be with someone who accepts me for who I am,
who isn't threatened by the fact that I'm an insatiably curious sex writer whose urine is arguably more valuable than
her ideas. I don't want someone to like me *despite* that—
I want someone to like me *because* of that. And I want
to be able to curb my jealousy and accept someone for
all their weird and vaguely annoying tendencies, too. (It's
only fair.) I want someone who respects my ideas about
sluthood, but who also is going to push me out of my
blindly defiant default setting and inspire me to be emotionally vulnerable. I want someone who challenges me,
but who also makes me feel deeply understood.

I think that, particularly in my generation, we've been
brought up to believe that independence and individual-
ity should be primary goals. We're told that if we want

to be a modern, hashtag liberated *Lean In* feminist, we should avoid shifting from being an "I" to a "we," and that we should resist changing ourselves for our partners—whether that means putting off monogamy, or prioritizing your career equally with your relationship, or not taking your husband's last name, or insisting that your boyfriend tolerate your taste for pink velvet furniture, or whatever. And, of course, independence is hugely important. But I think that sometimes, in the heat of this pursuit, we can forget the importance of love and partnership, and all the things you gain from being a team. At least, I know I can. Because truly, isn't the ideal that someone changes you for the better? That someone makes you feel happier, more supported, more known, and just generally like less of a manic bitch? I probably sound sappy, but I'm saying this because I want to make it clear that my goal in life is not simply to be an uncompromising slut maniac, or to assert that any person who won't accept me as is, sans negotiation, just isn't good enough or "enlightened" enough to be with me. Not at all. Truly, I want to be with someone who inspires me to be myself, but better. I want to take Christopher Ryan's advice and say, "This is who I am," while also being self-aware enough to know that there's obviously room for a touch-up once in a while.

Beyond that, I guess I don't really know what I want. I'm never going to be the type of person with a five-year plan. Honestly, if you told me that in five years I would be living uptown, married to a Wall Street dude, and blogging about being pregnant, I would believe you. On the other hand, I could also believe that in five years I'll be living in Mexico, in a poly relationship with a nongendered entity, running a hipster brothel. I just really don't know. Maybe life is like a craft fair embroidery wall ornament and we truly never know what we want until it's right in front of us. Or maybe we never know *ever*, and life is literally just an endless, mostly embarrassing journey of figuring ourselves out (especially if you're a narcissistic Millennial).

But one thing I know for certain, no matter whether I end up a Wall Street wife or a madam (or somewhere in between), is that I never want to get to a point where I look back on my sluttiness as being a "phase" that I've matured out of. That narrative is all too common. Often, we associate promiscuity with youth and bad decisions, and are expected to calm down (or slut down?) with age. Some people even begin to regret their promiscuous pasts. I'm often asked how I "deal" with the thought of getting older, and my potential future kids being able to find videos online of me shaving my vagina (for "art," but still), alongside old blog posts about the drug-fueled orgies of my early twenties. But I'm kind of insulted by the idea that just because I grow up, I should automatically reject my past and the things that were once important to me, as if the former and fluctuating incarnations of ourselves are not all valid parts of who we are. It's kind of like how if someone has a same-sex partner but then ultimately ends up in a heterosexual relationship, their bisexuality is often relegated to having been "just a phase." But why would that be true?

Why would a new relationship, or new desires, discredit our former experiences, loves, and orgasms? Surely the entirety of my sexuality does not hinge on the person who's inside me at this very moment. (Yes, I write with someone inside me—I told you that sluts are great at multitasking.) My sexuality is an ever-changing, oppressively complex labyrinth of beauty, nightmares, and transcendence, and it is mine and mine alone.

If you're reading the last page of this book first, you won't know that way back in the intro manifesto, I laid out my personal definition of a slut as a person who seeks out visceral experiences through sex. Being a slut means approaching sex in a way that's positive and additive to your life, free of the burden of social stigma. And that definition can apply to anyone, no matter their age, gender, or relationship status. Being a slut is a mind-set. It's a decision. And if there's one thing that I'm not noncommittal about, it's that I choose to live life in a sluttier state of consciousness.

rejected book titles

The Slut Also Rises

Slut and the City

Being Offended, and
Other Essays

Snatch Antics

Cuntsulting

Lesbian Nightmare Festival

Cliterature

Vageneral Interest

Whoreality

The Slut's Guide to the
Galaxy

Vagenda

Cunting Linguist

The Little Pink Book
(of Amorality)

On Sluttiness

Whore and Peen

Cum As You Are

The Slut Also Smizes

Holita

How to Lose Your
Dignity in 10 Days

The Slutyssey

Moby Dick

Skank-Lit

Trigger Warning

The Slut and the Fury

The Sisterhood of the
Traveling Skanks

Lez Jizerables

Madam Ovary

acknowledgments

To my family, for loving me, putting up with me, and for fucking me up in all the right ways. To Sally Singer, for taking a chance and giving the slut blogger a column at *Vogue*. To Andrew Richardson, for years of slutty wisdom, as off-base as you can be at times. To Maddie Caldwell, my editor at Grand Central, for your invaluable guidance, and for making me sound like less of an idiot. To my agent, Luke Janklow, for all of your support, and for fielding my manic phone calls with grace and depth of voice. To Max Stein, because you (weirdly) seem to care about my success more than I do. To Kelsi, because you're my personal slutty heroine (and because it's always good to have a friend who's sluttier than you). To Sophia Larigakis, for helping me organize my thoughts (and words), and for your unequivocally Gen Z feedback. To Zach, for taking me to the top of the Empire State Building on the night that I *finally* finished this book (and for the many other times that you've made me feel high, literally and figuratively). To probiotics, for helping to keep my pH in check through it all—I know it hasn't been easy for you. And to all the sluts out there: You are loved.

about the author

Karley Sciortino is a writer, television journalist, and producer, based in New York and Los Angeles. She is the founder of Slutever, a website that explores sexuality and attempts to be both funny and insightful. She also writes Vogue.com's sex and relationships column, Breathless, and is the creator and host of *Slutever*, a documentary TV series on Viceland that explores sexual behavior. She is also a regular contributor to *Purple* magazine.